Biscuit *Bliss*

Biscuit *Bliss*

101 Foolproof Recipes for Fresh and Fluffy Biscuits in Just Minutes

James Villas

THE HARVARD COMMON PRESS

Boston, Massachusetts

The Harvard Common Press
535 Albany Street
Boston, Massachusetts 02118

Printed in the United States of America

Library of Congress Cataloging-in-Publication Data
Villas, James
  Biscuit bliss : 101 foolproof recipes for fresh and fluffy biscuits in
just minutes / James Villas.
        p. cm.
Includes index.
  ISBN 1-55832-222-1 (hc : alk. paper) — ISBN 1-55832-223-X
(pb : alk. paper)
  1. Biscuits. I. Title.
  TX770.B55.V55 2004
  641.9'15—dc22   2003019438

978-1-55832-223-3

Special bulk-order discounts are available on this and other Harvard
Common Press books. Companies and organizations may purchase
books for premiums or resale, or may arrange a custom edition, by
contacting the Marketing Director at the address above.

10 9 8 7 6 5 4

Cover and interior design by Night & Day Design
Photographs by Alexandra Grablewski
Food styling by Megan Fawn Schlow

For Mary "Mac" Mahone

----

*a gracious Southern lady,
an amazing cook, and a generous,
beloved friend*

Contents

Acknowledgments

Having been weaned on biscuits in the South, I wish I could say that this book was my idea. The credit, however, must go to my longtime Yankee editor at The Harvard Common Press, Pam Hoenig, whose passion for baking and eating biscuits is surpassed only by her uncanny ability to catch every single mistake in my recipes.

My sincere appreciation to Linda Carman at Martha White Kitchens in Nashville, Tennessee, the quintessential "biscuit lady" whose help has been invaluable; and without regular shipments of superior Southern flour from the folks at White Lily in Knoxville, Tennessee, testing so many biscuit recipes wouldn't have been half as successful. For special advice, ideas, tips, and recipes, I also thank Shirley Corriher, Jean Anderson, and Damon Lee Fowler. Equally cooperative have been the enthusiasts at City Tavern in Philadelphia, Crooks Corner in Chapel Hill, North Carolina, Hay Day Market in Westport, Connecticut, and Chanterelle restaurant in Manhattan, not to mention the dozens of faded names and faces from Roanoke, Virginia, to Green Bay, Wisconsin, to Monterey, California, who over the many years, have shared recipes and cooking techniques and demonstrated what a regional phenomenon biscuit and scone making really is. Finally a big peck on the cheek to the greatest biscuit expert of them all, namely my Southern mother, Martha Pearl Villas, who still says I don't know a thing about making perfect biscuits.

Introduction

The Romance of Biscuits

As if it were just yesterday, I can still see my great-aunt in North Carolina making a fresh batch of buttermilk biscuits for breakfast. On the counter was a big wooden bowl into which she'd dumped an entire five-pound sack of flour a day or so earlier and kept covered with a towel. When she was ready, Aunt Toots would simply make a well in the center with her fingers, add unmeasured quantities of baking powder, baking soda, and salt to the indention, whisk it all around with just the right eyeful of flour collected from the sides of the bowl, and quickly rub small scoops of lard into the mixture till it was mealy. Next, she'd add just enough buttermilk from a jug to make a sticky dough, pat out perfect rounds with her floured hands, arrange them almost touching one another on a heavy, slightly battered baking sheet, and stick them in the hot oven.

She'd then re-cover the utterly dry remaining flour intended for more biscuits at suppertime and proceed to fry bacon while the biscuits were baking. The entire mixing and patting procedure took maybe five minutes. Aunt Toots never once looked at a clock or even peeked in the oven, and when she knew instinctively the biscuits were ready, she'd simply hand me a dish cloth while she stirred a pot of grits and direct, "Take 'em out honey—now!" As always, the biscuits were high and fluffy, the tops golden brown and slightly knobby, and, when I broke one open to butter the halves, the soft, moist inside released a tangy aroma that almost made me salivate. The flavor was indescribable.

Since those childhood days, I've watched my own mother turn out thousands of amazing biscuits, I've made countless batches myself, and sampled every style imaginable from coast to coast, but, for whatever sentimental or psychological reasons, I don't think I've ever tasted biscuits quite like those flaky, sapid wonders that Aunt Toots concocted—and it's for sure I've never again seen anybody duplicate her amazing method of dealing so deftly with all that flour. Like most Southerners, of course, I've been obsessed with biscuits my entire life, a passion no doubt inherited from generations of family and relatives like Aunt Toots and one that serves as the major inspiration for this book. Since biscuits have been prepared and loved throughout America ever since the country was founded, I'm not about to insinuate that Rebels have a monopoly on the bread. But it is true that, historically and gastronomically, biscuits have been as much part of the South's cultural backbone as pork barbecue and fruit cobblers, and that just the

idea of going two or three days without some form of biscuit is literally inconceivable to me when I'm home.

Southerners certainly didn't invent biscuits, but we do claim them atavistically as a major component of our natural birthright. Actually the term biscuit derives from the Latin *bis* ("twice") plus *coctus* ("cooked") and refers most likely to a crude Roman bread made in the first century A.D. During the Middle Ages, the English developed their first savory *bysquytes* and the Scots their closely related sweetened and unsweetened *skonns* (scones), and by the late seventeenth and early eighteenth centuries in France there had evolved a *pain bis-cuit* ("twice-baked bread"), which, like the British examples, was probably an unleavened, dry, hard flatbread or cracker cooked first on a griddle, then baked and used as a spoilage-resistant ration for military troops on the move. No doubt it was these rudimentary, long-lasting styles of biscuit (or "ship's biscuit") that were part of the provisions on both ships headed for colonial America and the first whaling boats of New England. In 1828, Webster defined biscuit as "a composition of flour and butter, made and baked in private families," but it was not till a few years later, with the introduction of baking soda, that the small, leavened, puffy, American-style "soda biscuit" (in contrast to the unleavened cracker type) began to resemble the biscuits we know today. All that was needed next was commercial baking powder and yeast, which made their first appearances in 1856 and 1868 respectively and revolutionized a

biscuit bonus

Always use vegetable shortening or lard to grease a baking sheet for biscuits. Butter tends to make them stick and the bottoms overbrown.

bread that would take America—and especially the South—by storm.

Of course, much of the history of American biscuits is shrouded in mystery and conjecture, one puzzle being the origins of a "beaten biscuit," which was probably the American original and which seems to have been popular throughout the Eastern states long before baking soda, baking powder, and yeast came along. Unleavened biscuits made with flour, lard, and milk that were beaten repeatedly with a pestle, heavy mallet, or skillet to soften and smooth them might well have been a common staple in home kitchens as far back as the mid-eighteenth century. Essentially, the biscuits were continuously layered and pounded to introduce air into the dough and give them a lift in the oven, but so laborious and time-consuming was the practice that eventually it was up to a woman in Vineland, New Jersey (a Yankee!), to come up with a rather primitive dough-kneading machine through which the dough could be passed over and over till it was light and smooth. Then, later on in the nineteenth century, a manufacturer in Missouri invented a beaten biscuit brake with two nickel-plated rollers that made the job even easier and the biscuits even more popular. With all the advantages of both biological and chemical leavenings to producing fluffy raised biscuits, the tradition of making firm, dry, smooth beaten biscuits (or, as they curiously also came to be called, Maryland biscuits) was gradually relegated to a few Southern states, and while today the old art has almost disap-

biscuit bonus

When rubbing chilled fat into biscuit dough, work quickly so that the heat from your fingers doesn't melt the fat and produce an undesirable oily, flakeless biscuit.

peared, there are still enthusiasts (especially in Kentucky) who own biscuit brakes and wouldn't dream of making biscuits any other way.

Whether twentieth-century cooks chose to beat their biscuits the old-fashioned way or utilize the more practical leavenings, it's for sure that with the advent of commercial biscuit mixes like Bisquick in the 1930s and canned biscuits in the 1940s, a century-old art that had been the province of kitchens all over America was changed forever in favor of facility and with little regard for distinctive flavor and texture. Soon these bogus products filled the cases of every supermarket. Some were used as a foundation for everything from frozen meat pies to pizzas to fried "dogs on a stick," and it wasn't long before modern fast-food outlets everywhere were touting standardized biscuits in every guise possible on their menus. Little wonder that by the present age, fresh home-baked biscuits have virtually disappeared from most kitchens outside the South, and even in that region, which has fostered tradition like none other, biscuit making is hardly the same widespread ritual it was when I was growing up in North Carolina.

The irony, of course, is not only that I've never met a human soul who didn't relish, indeed rave about, freshly baked biscuits, but that no bread is simpler, quicker, and more downright fun to make. As this book is intended to illustrate, the regional diversity of biscuits (and scones) is both fascinating and revealing of our rich heritage; the flexibility of ingredients and techniques is enough to reassure even the most nervous cook; and so long as you respect a few basic time-tested rules (e. g., adding the right amount of baking powder in proportion to the style of flour used, rubbing or cutting fats quickly into the flour mixtures, using the right equipment, and, above all, never overmixing the dough), there's really no reason why biscuit making can't add a whole new dimension to cozy breakfasts and elaborate weekend brunches, to stylish afternoon teas and cocktail parties, to informal cookouts and picnics, and even to the snazziest suppers. Then, once you've mastered the knack of turning out great biscuits and scones for almost every occasion imaginable, there's also a chapter devoted to the many clever and lip-smacking ways that biscuits and biscuit doughs can be utilized to make or enhance all sorts of main-course dishes and sumptuous desserts.

Although the exact origins and much of the lore surrounding American biscuits remain obscure, I have every reason to believe that this simple, distinctive, and delectable bread has played an important role in virtually every step of the country's development. Subjected to numerous transformations by the original European settlers, no doubt one style of biscuit or another nourished our colonial ancestors, the explorers and fishermen who depended on such practical staples for survival in the wilderness and at sea, and, to be sure, the

biscuit bonus

The amount of liquid needed to produce ideal biscuit dough is always variable and can depend on the style of flour used. Generally, add enough liquid to make the dough very soft, often wet and sticky, unless the recipe directions indicate otherwise.

early pioneers and cowboys who baked their sourdough biscuits three times a day in chuckwagon Dutch ovens over open fires. As the nation developed, every region, exploiting its own flours, meals, fats, leavenings, and indigenous secondary ingredients, evolved different ways of making biscuits, resulting in a repertory that is as eclectic today as it was a century ago.

Most of these diverse ingredients and cooking techniques are represented in the book, explanation enough of why some recipes utilize certain flours and fats, others call for different quantities of baking powder and liquid to make specific types of dough, and still others indicate oven temperatures and baking times that are not consistent with the norm. Quite frankly, I don't think I've ever once made a batch of biscuits the exact same way, and once you've mastered the basic techniques and determined your personal likes and dislikes, I strongly encourage you, within reason, to give full rein to your instincts. Try all sorts of flours, fats, and liquids, experiment with dough textures, vary the sizes and shapes of the biscuits, test alternate baking procedures, and, of course, never stop thinking of sensible ingredients and flavorings that might enhance your biscuits—and, consequently, make the recipes your own. That's what the romance of biscuits is all about, and that's what links us to a long, bold, proud regional tradition that must never be allowed to disappear.

Biscuit Basics

N o cooking activity is easier and more fun than baking a successful batch of biscuits, so long, that is, as you respect the ingredients, use the right equipment, and observe a few basic procedures that are as valid today as a century ago. Take a moment to carefully review the following fundamentals before measuring ingredients, sticking your hands in the dough, cutting out rounds, and placing the baking sheet in the oven. It could make all the difference in the way your biscuits come out.

INGREDIENTS

The three basic ingredients of biscuits couldn't be simpler, but since each can have a dramatic effect on baking success, special attention should be paid.

Flours

Wheat flours can be unbleached or bleached, meaning that, during the milling process, either the whole grain (including the germ) is ground (unbleached) or both the outer coat and germ of the grain are removed (bleached) to facilitate processing and assure longer shelf life for the flour. The main difference between the two is that unbleached flour has higher nutritional value and, some believe, better taste. To restore nutrients to bleached flours, millers "enrich" them with various vitamins and minerals. In general, all-purpose flour, bleached or unbleached, is enriched and can be used interchangeably when making biscuits and most other breads.

Although you can certainly make delectable biscuits with ordinary all-purpose flour (a blend of soft and hard wheats), one of the undebatable truths of this world is that nothing produces more wondrous biscuits than soft winter wheat Southern flour. (To test the notion, all you have to do is make two batches of biscuits side by side using the separate flours and observe the differences in height and fluffiness.) The main reason is that Southern flour contains less gluten-forming proteins than the hard-wheat flours found in most other areas of the country and the different ways the flours react with baking powder. Hard-wheat flours might be ideal for yeast-leavened breads, but for biscuits, which depend on quick-acting chemical leaveners, nothing guarantees ideal results like soft Southern flour.

Reducing the gluten-forming protein in all-purpose flour by substituting in part some soft cake flour is often one acceptable option for certain biscuits, but if you're really serious about biscuit making, you'll seek out such superior Southern flours as White Lily, Martha White, Red Band, and Melrose. Few of these flours are widely available outside the South (White Lily is marketed nationwide in most Williams-Sonoma shops), but two can now be ordered in five-pound bags directly from the producers, and a very good soft-wheat pastry flour suitable for biscuits is available from a third source in the North. Check the mail-order source section at the back of the book.

Self-rising flour is simply enriched all-purpose flour to which baking powder and salt have been added. Although most of today's self-rising flours can be effectively substituted for regular all-purpose flour (minus, of course, any baking powder and salt asked for in your recipe), many cooks don't trust them since, during delays in merchandizing or storing, the leavening can lose some of its potency. I always have both types of flour on hand for making biscuits and think all serious biscuit makers should too. Just make sure you check the expiration date stamped on the bags of self-rising flour. Frankly, my biscuits turn out just as well with self-rising as with all-purpose flour—and no doubt the former is quicker when you're in a hurry.

biscuit bonus

To make your own self-rising flour (enough for about a dozen biscuits), sift together into a bowl 1¼ cups bleached all-purpose flour, ¾ cup cake flour (or use only all-purpose flour), 4 teaspoons baking powder, and 1 teaspoon salt. Store larger amounts in an airtight canister up to two months.

Leavenings

American Indians in the eighteenth century learned to use pearl ash to lighten their crude breads, but it was not till the mid-nineteenth century, when commercial baking soda (1840), commercial baking powder (1856), and commercial yeast (1868) were introduced, that cooks began to leaven their biscuits into the fluffy wonders they became in the twentieth century. Today, there are a few styles of biscuit leavened with slow-acting yeast or cream of tartar (a powdered, fast-acting acid salt), but by far the two most standard agents are chemical baking powders and baking soda, both of which are alkaline compounds used in conjunction with acidic ingredients to quickly produce the carbon dioxide gas necessary to make biscuits porous and light and to coax them to rise highly when baked.

Baking soda can be the sole leavening for biscuits if the dough is acidic enough to react with it and generate carbon dioxide, but most biscuits depend primarily on baking powders for fast rising and lightness. Although there are single-acting baking powders, which are ideal for fine-textured cakes and other delicate baked goods, biscuits always call for the double-acting type, which produces an initial set of gas bubbles when the powder comes into contact with the liquid, then a second set during the baking process. Using too little baking powder will prevent biscuits from rising properly, but too much can not only produce a chemical aftertaste but also make the biscuits too dry. I usually try to gauge the quantity of baking powder according to the style of flour being used and the amount of acidic ingredients in the recipe, but rarely do I use more than a full tablespoon of baking powder per 2 cups of flour.

Always check the expiration date on a can of baking powder. To test whether the powder has lost all or part of its potency drop ½ teaspoon of it into a glass of warm water. If it foams vigorously, the powder is still fully active. If it is over the hill and you're caught in a dilemma, remember that you can always make your own baking powder by combining roughly equal amounts of baking soda and cream of tartar. And never forget that if you dip a wet spoon into a baking powder can, you'll deactivate the entire can.

biscuit bonus

To avoid any chemical aftertaste of commercial baking powder, you can make your own by combining equal amounts of baking soda and cream of tartar. Store the mixture in a tightly sealed container up to two months.

Although baking soda by itself has no leavening properties and must be used in combination with acid ingredients such as buttermilk or molasses to be effective, it can produce very tender biscuits. The proportion of baking soda to liquid is about 1 teaspoon soda to 1 cup of liquid, the reaction being basically the same as when the acid and alkaline in baking powder come in contact with liquid to produce carbon dioxide. For this reason, be sure to first mix baking soda with dry ingredients before adding any liquid.

Active dry yeast (proofed in warm water or not proofed) can be used with or without other leavenings to produce biscuits that are particularly light and fluffy, but I think it's misleading to suggest that yeast automatically guarantees a feathery biscuit or necessarily a superior one—just too many other important factors are involved. I rarely resort to yeast in biscuit cookery since I much prefer the sturdy but light textures produced by baking powder and baking soda. I can't deny, on the other hand, that a double-leavened angel biscuit can be one of the best breads on earth when made properly, and classic Jewish yeast biscuits just wouldn't be the same leavened with other agents. Do be sure to buy baker's active dry yeast (in ¼-ounce packets or 4-ounce jars) and not brewer's yeast, which is *not* a leavener but used mainly for brewing beer. Kept in a cool, dry area, active dry yeast maintains its potency at least three months.

Fats

Lard (the rendered fat of hogs), vegetable shortening, butter, and margarine are the principal fats used to make biscuits and each has its own distinctive properties. Their function is not only to impart flavor, but, most important, to grease the proteins present in the flour so that the liquids cannot activate the gluten; to separate the flakes in doughs by melting between the starchy layers during baking; and to thus tenderize (shorten) the overall texture of the biscuits.

There can be no doubt that lard, which is 100 percent fat, produces the fleeciest, most tender biscuits since it has the greatest shortening power and maintains the biscuit's crisp texture at all temperatures. (Curiously enough, however, pure lard contains considerably less cholesterol than butter.) Next best for fluffiness is vegetable shortening, constituted of both animal and vegetable oils and today the most popular fat for making biscuits. Butter and margarine are both richer in flavor, but since they are only 80 percent fat, they have less shortening power than lard or vegetable shortening and thus yield a heavier texture (especially butter, because of its milk solids).

The ultimate biscuit, of course, would have the combined flaky tenderness produced by lard, the fluffiness from vegetable shortening, and the rich flavor of butter. Mixing fats is always an option, but be warned that it can be risky if you're not familiar (through experience) with how each behaves. Just a little flavorful butter, for example, can reduce the flakiness of biscuits made primarily with lard or vegetable shortening, and although combining butter and margarine will lower a butter biscuit's cholesterol, both the flavor and possibly the texture will be noticeably affected. The best idea is simply to experiment, recording your amounts and results each time.

> **biscuit bonus**
>
> *For the flakiest biscuits, chill the butter, shortening, or lard and quickly rub it (or cut it with a pastry cutter) into the flour before adding the other ingredients.*

Note also that, because of its high butterfat content, heavy cream by itself can be used to moisten and shorten some biscuits without the help of another fat. (Light cream or half-and-half will *not* do the job properly.) As for substituting a cooking oil for a fat, I have included one recipe in this book that utilizes olive oil (with somewhat questionable results), but, generally, I advise strongly against the practice unless you're willing to risk ending up with oily, tough biscuits.

I always store lard, like butter and margarine, in the refrigerator since it can become rancid. I've heard or read somewhere that vegetable shortening tends to break down if it's kept chilled, but I've never once had that problem. Perhaps it's because I use only Crisco.

BISCUIT-BAKING EQUIPMENT

Biscuit making requires only the most rudimentary, relatively inexpensive cooking equipment, but every item is important and rarely should substitutions be made if optimum results are expected. To mix the dough, a large, deep bowl with plenty of wide surface area is obligatory for rapid whisking of the dry ingredients, cutting in the fat, and easy stirring of the dough. I use three different mixing bowls, one heavy wooden, another stainless steel, and the third a sturdy ceramic produced by Arm & Hammer exclusively for making biscuits. Since aluminum can give acidic ingredients a metallic taste unless it is well anodized, I shy away from these bowls.

Nothing is more strategic in biscuit making than baking sheets and pans, the color, size, and gauge of which must be right for ideal results. Shiny baking sheets are preferred by far to dark ones since dark surfaces absorb heat more quickly and could cause overbrowning of the bottoms. All my baking sheets for biscuits measure 13 to 15 inches by 10 inches and, for even heat distribution, all are rimless lengthwise, with only a slight lip on each end. (Be warned that, for some reason, rimless baking sheets are increasingly difficult to find even in the finest shops and hardware stores.) A thin, light, flimsy baking sheet is worthless for baking biscuits intended to have uniform color and texture, so buy the heaviest gauge you can find (the sheet should not bend in the least). As for nonstick sheets and pans, experiment carefully till you determine how quickly and evenly they bake. And for biscuits to be baked in a cast-iron skillet, just make sure to use only skillets that are kept well seasoned by being periodically heated with a little oil on the surface in a preheated 300°F oven for about 30 minutes.

A half-moon-shaped stainless-steel pastry cutter is essential for cutting fats evenly into flour mixtures and for stirring doughs, I use only heavy wooden spoons or a large, heavy fork. For me, it would be inconceivable to make biscuits without legitimate sharp, metal, small-handled biscuit cutters, and my prized collection ranges in sizes from $1\frac{1}{2}$ to $3\frac{1}{2}$ inches. Since these cutters almost guarantee even biscuits, promote rising by not sealing the edges, and are not expensive, I can't understand why anybody would use a dull juice glass, rough tin can, or any other inferior substitute to cut out biscuits.

BISCUIT PERFECTION

While there are certain principles governing the correct preparation of beaten biscuits, drop biscuits, tea biscuits, and other styles (enumerated where applicable throughout this book), special attention should be paid here to perfecting traditional baking powder biscuits since these are by far the most popular throughout America and the ones you're most likely to serve on a regular basis. In general, perfect baking powder biscuits should be at least one inch high with even or slightly

"Let's talk about biscuits. Southern biscuits. Buttermilk biscuits so hot that you can grab one but not hold it longer than it takes to move from tray to plate. The top is a perfect circle, burnished gold, oven-crisp. The bottom is a darker disk, thicker from contact with the baking sheet. And the columnar side is snow white, as tender as sifted flour. Give a gentle tug, and it pulls apart like a warm cloud. Now quickly grab pats of butter, ease them on, ever so meekly, and watch the cleaved biscuits drink in the fast-melting yellow emulsion. Honey? Jam? Sorghum molasses? Redeye gravy? Yes, yes, yes, yes. Everything is good on biscuits."

—JANE AND MICHAEL STERN, *A Taste of America*, 1988

craggy tops, light golden brown outside, flaky and slightly moist and fluffy inside, light and tender in texture, and clean tasting. Of course, the rules for making such biscuits successfully can vary from region to region and from cook to cook, but I do have my own strong convictions about a number of points.

1. I don't think there's any procedure in cooking I loathe more or consider less necessary than sifting flour. Particularly in the case of biscuits, there's simply no reason to ever sift when a whisk can be used more quickly and efficiently to mix the ingredients evenly and break up any lumps.

2. One of the worst mistakes you can make with biscuits is to premix all the ingredients and allow the dough to stand for even a short amount of time—even in the refrigerator—before baking. It is indeed perfectly safe to premix the dry ingredients, but since the first action of the double-acting baking powder occurs the moment liquid is added (the second is when it's exposed to high heat), you want to maximize the leavening by getting the mixed and cut biscuits in the oven as quickly as possible. For high, fluffy biscuits, never mix the dough completely and let it sit and, likewise,

never cut out biscuits till you're ready to pop them into the hot oven.

3. Perhaps the most important rule in biscuit making is that the dough should be handled as little as possible to prevent toughness—minimum stirring of ingredients, kneading the dough no more than a few strokes, and gentle rolling or patting out.

4. The ideal biscuit dough should be slightly wet and sticky after mixing. It might seem awfully messy, but it is this consistency of dough that produces the crispiest and fluffiest biscuits. When working with such a dough, I keep my fingers (or rolling pin) very lightly floured to minimize the stickiness.

5. Rolling out dough might produce a smoother surface on biscuits, but since the natural tendency is to over-roll, I almost always simply pat mine out as gently as possible. It's quicker, easier, and, besides, I actually prefer biscuits that are a bit craggy on top. Without exception, biscuits that are patted instead of rolled out also seem more tender.

6. Cutting out biscuits is very important, and nobody should be without a sturdy, sharp, metal biscuit cutter. A small juice glass can be used in emergencies, but remember that since this does not allow air to escape during the cutting, the biscuit can be overly compressed. To avoid jagged edges on biscuits (and uneven baking of the sides), never twist the cutter—simply cut straight down in one quick stroke.

7. The best baking sheets for biscuits are heavy, sturdy, metal ones with no lips except for on one side (often difficult to find today for some strange reason). If the sheet is too

biscuit bonus

Unbaked biscuits can be frozen successfully up to one month without losing their texture. Freeze the rounds immediately after cutting them out in a single layer on a baking sheet, then wrap in aluminum foil, and transfer to freezer bags. When ready to bake, do not thaw; simply double the cooking time of fresh biscuits.

thin and flimsy, the bottoms of the biscuits can burn, and if it has lips on all sides, the biscuits might not bake evenly. So long as there's adequate fat in the biscuit dough, there's no need to grease the baking sheet.

8. If you like your biscuits browned all over, bake them about 1 inch apart on the baking sheet. Personally, I prefer the sides of most biscuits to be rather soft, so to keep the sides from overbrowning, I generally space the biscuits about 1/2 inch apart.

9. Biscuits must be baked only in a preheated oven so that the high heat forces the baking powder to act immediately. I either preheat the oven to 450°F and bake the biscuits 10 to 12 minutes, or to 425°F for 12 to 14 minutes—depending on exactly what texture I want. Do remember, however, that the calibration of ovens can differ radically and that often a bit of experimentation is necessary before you can establish the right temperature and baking time.

10. Leftover biscuits, for me, are not very good reheated, but when they're split (never cut open with a knife!), buttered, and toasted, they're utterly delicious for breakfast and almost as good as freshly baked ones. Biscuits stored in airtight plastic bags will keep well when refrigerated about four days, and they can be frozen for up to a month without losing much of their moisture.

BISCUIT TROUBLE-SHOOTING

Problem	Possible Cause	Problem	Possible Cause
Didn't rise high enough	• Not enough baking powder • Overmixing of dough • Oven too hot	Tough	• Not enough baking powder or baking soda • Placed biscuits too close together on baking sheet • Overmixing of dough
Not flaky	• Not enough fat in dough • Too much butter and not enough shortening or lard • Overmixing of dough	Not even and smooth	• Used blunt biscuit cutter • Biscuit cutter twisted while cutting
Not light and fluffy	• Dough was not wet and sticky enough • Overmixing of dough • Used blunt biscuit cutter	Hard bottoms	• Baking sheet too thin or dark • Baking sheet greased with butter • Oven rack set too low
Too dry	• Too much baking powder • Baked too long	Chemical taste	• Too much baking powder

Plain Raised Biscuits

Another name for these plain raised biscuits could be Everyday Biscuits, meaning the ones that cooks throughout America have been making on a fairly regular basis for the past two centuries. These are the simple biscuits that, in one form or another, have served as part of the foundation of classic American cookery, the ones on which our ancestors were nourished, and the ones that continue to grace tables in homes (and restaurants) all across the regions. Some are the light, fluffy, tender wonders that have come to typify the ideal American biscuit; others are the denser examples that go so well with full-flavored soups, stews, and other hearty dishes; and a few are the relatively dry, crunchy rascals that many prefer at backyard cookouts and picnics and that seem to keep forever.

Essentially, most of these raised biscuits are made from a traditional flour or meal dough that is leavened with baking powder, shortened with fat, and moistened with some type of liquid. After that, all rules go out the window as biscuit aficionados from all over assert their authority: they demand certain flours, fats, and liquids; insist upon different ingredient proportions; debate mixing techniques; and defend stances on baking temperature, exactly where the biscuits should be placed in the oven, and, of course, how long they should be baked. Needless to say, I, like any crusty Southerner, have my own staunch theories on every aspect of biscuit making, but I do at least try to keep an open mind and experiment as much as possible. You'll therefore notice many slight recipe variants in this chapter, all illustrating different regional concepts and practices, but all, as I see it, only adding to the wide diversity and overall excitement of making good biscuits.

Traditional Baking Powder Biscuits

This has been my (and my Southern mother's) basic way of making everyday biscuits for as long as I can remember. Soft Southern flour milled from winter wheat, of course, produces the highest, fluffiest biscuit, but I certainly have no objections to making these biscuits with either ordinary white all-purpose or very fresh self-rising flour (minus the baking powder and part of the salt) when I run out of White Lily, Red Band, or Martha White. What's most important is to add just enough milk to make a slightly sticky dough, and *not* to stir or knead the dough too much. If the biscuits do not rise at least one inch after baking, check to make sure the date stamped on the baking powder tin has not passed. I also love these biscuits split, buttered, and toasted for breakfast.

Makes about 16 biscuits

2 cups all-purpose flour
1 tablespoon baking powder
1 teaspoon salt
¹/₄ cup chilled vegetable shortening
³/₄ to 1 cup whole milk, as needed

1. Preheat the oven to 425°F.

2. In a large mixing bowl, whisk together the flour, baking powder, and salt. Add the shortening and cut it in with a pastry cutter or rub with your fingertips till the mixture is mealy. Gradually add the milk, stirring with a fork, just till the dough holds together and is still sticky.

3. Transfer the dough to a lightly floured work surface, knead about 8 times, pat out ¹/₂ inch thick, and cut out rounds with a 2-inch biscuit cutter. Pat the scraps together and cut out more rounds.

4. Arrange the rounds on a baking sheet about 1 inch apart and bake in the upper third of the oven till golden brown, about 15 minutes.

biscuit bonus

Never substitute bread flour for all-purpose flour when making biscuits since the high percentage of gluten-forming protein in bread flour causes biscuits to toughen.

Three-Fat Baking Powder Biscuits

In many respects, this is the ideal baking powder biscuit since the lard yields a delightfully brittle texture, the shortening a delicate fluffiness, and the butter a rich flavor. Just make sure that the lard is not rancid and that all the fats are slightly chilled before cutting or rubbing them into the flour.

Makes about 16 biscuits

2 cups all-purpose flour
1 tablespoon baking powder
1 teaspoon salt
2 tablespoons chilled lard
2 tablespoons chilled vegetable shortening
1 tablespoon chilled butter
1 cup whole milk

1. Preheat the oven to 425°F.

2. In a large mixing bowl, whisk together the flour, baking powder, and salt. Add the lard, shortening, and butter and cut them in with a pastry cutter or rub with your fingertips till the mixture is mealy. Make a well in the center, add the milk, and stir briskly with a fork just till the dough holds together.

3. Transfer the dough to a lightly floured work surface, knead about 8 times, pat out 1/2 inch thick, and cut out rounds with a 2-inch biscuit cutter. Pat the scraps together and cut out more rounds.

4. Arrange the rounds on a baking sheet 1 inch apart for crusty-sided biscuits or almost touching for soft ones and bake in the upper third of the oven till golden brown, about 15 minutes.

Homemade Biscuit Mix

Long before various baking mixes were packaged and placed on supermarket shelves, our ancestors concocted their own convenience mixtures of flour, baking powder, salt, and fat, which were stored for long periods and used to make biscuits every day, as well as muffins, pancakes, coffee cakes, and virtually any other quick bread product that today might call for a commercial mix. I've taken up this habit and suggest you do the same in preparation for having to make biscuits at the last minute and not wanting to fool with measuring ingredients. As a safeguard against bugs and rancid shortening, be sure to store the mixture in an airtight canister in the refrigerator, where it keeps for weeks and weeks. When the time comes to make quick biscuits, all you have to do is add liquid to the measured mixture, pat out the dough, form or cut out biscuits, and bake away.

12 cups all-purpose flour
6 tablespoons baking powder
6 teaspoons salt
3 cups chilled vegetable shortening

1. In a very large mixing bowl, whisk together the flour, baking powder, and salt. Add the shortening and cut with a pastry cutter till the mixture is mealy, almost granular.

2. Transfer to an airtight canister and store in the refrigerator till you're ready to make biscuits.

Makes about 4 quarts of mix

Mother's Buttermilk Biscuits

For many Southerners, this is the queen of all biscuits, and my North Carolina mother is no exception. These are the light, fluffy, tangy wonders that nurtured me as a child, the ones featured at barbecues, church suppers, and political rallies throughout the South, and the ones I still make on a fairly regular basis. Needless to say, Mother couldn't imagine making these biscuits with anything but soft, low-gluten, winter Southern flour and Crisco shortening, and to watch her fix a batch following no "receipt" except the one in her head and fingers is a unique experience I've yet to duplicate with total success. By no means should you handle this dough too much, and since the nature of all ovens can vary enormously, begin watching the biscuits very carefully after about 12 minutes to make sure the tops don't overbrown.

Makes about 16 biscuits

2 cups all-purpose flour
1 tablespoon baking powder
$1/2$ teaspoon baking soda
$1/2$ teaspoon salt
$1/4$ cup chilled vegetable shortening
1 cup buttermilk

1. Preheat the oven to 450°F.

2. In a large mixing bowl, whisk together the flour, baking powder, baking soda, and salt. Add the shortening and cut it in with a pastry cutter or rub with your fingertips till the mixture is mealy. Gradually add the buttermilk, stirring with a wooden spoon just till the dough is soft and slightly sticky.

3. Transfer the dough to a lightly floured work surface and, using a light touch, turn the edges toward the middle, pressing with your hands. Press the dough out $1/2$ inch thick and cut straight down into even rounds with a 2-inch biscuit cutter. Pat the scraps together and cut out more rounds.

4. Arrange the rounds on a baking sheet no more than $1/2$ inch apart and bake in the upper third of the oven till lightly browned on top, about 12 minutes.

biscuit bonus

If soft, low-protein Southern flour is unavailable for making biscuits, an acceptable substitute can be made by combining 2 parts all-purpose flour with 1 part cake flour.

Food Processor Beaten Biscuits

Although I've always believed that using a food processor takes the fun out of making most biscuits, I had to admit that my old friend and colleague Jeanne Voltz's method of shortening the lengthy procedure normally involved in producing beaten biscuits made lots of sense. Do notice that the dough is "tenderized" in a plastic bag for two hours before being beaten in the food processor, and that it is made even more supple by being rolled in layers repeatedly.

Makes about 1½ dozen biscuits

2 cups all-purpose flour
1 tablespoon sugar
½ teaspoon baking powder
½ teaspoon salt
¼ cup chilled lard
½ cup half-and-half

1. In a large mixing bowl, whisk together the flour, sugar, baking powder, and salt. Add the lard and rub it in with your fingertips till the mixture is mealy. Add the half-and-half and stir just till a loose dough forms. Gather up the dough into a ball, place in a plastic bag, and let stand for about 2 hours.

2. Preheat the oven to 325°F.

3. Divide the ball of dough into 2 portions and, using a food processor fitted with a plastic dough blade, process each portion for 2 minutes. Gather both portions together, place on a lightly floured work surface, and roll out ¼ inch thick. Fold over, roll out again, and continue folding and rolling till the dough is silky smooth, 4 to 6 times. After folding the final time, do not roll out. Cut out rounds with a 1½-inch biscuit cutter, refold the scraps, and cut out more rounds.

4. Arrange the rounds on a baking sheet about ½ inch apart and prick each round with a fork. Bake in the center of the oven till very pale brown and the insides are dry and flaky, about 25 minutes. Serve immediately or let cool completely and store in a tightly covered tin up to 1 week.

> *"My Mississippi mother, a Southern belle if ever there was one, loved beaten biscuits and served them often when she had friends over for afternoon coffee or tea. Outside the room in which I slept, there was the sawed-off, wide circular stump of a walnut tree, and it was there, early in the morning, that I could hear the beating of that biscuit dough, whack after whack after whack."*
> —CRAIG CLAIBORNE, *Southern Cooking*, 1987

Maryland Beaten Biscuits

Why these small, dry, crisp biscuits, which were staples aboard early whaling ships, are identified with the state of Maryland is a mystery since, for centuries, they've been just as popular not only in Virginia and Kentucky but throughout coastal New England (where they're often referred to as "sea biscuits"). No doubt this was the original American savory biscuit, conceived long before the convenience of baking powder and baking soda, when the only means of leavening was to beat the dough hard and repeatedly with a rolling pin, hammer, or side of an axe till it blistered and turned incredibly smooth.

Altogether different from their light, fluffy counterparts, beaten biscuits are fun to make and will keep up to a month in an airtight container. Just remember that they must be whacked at least 15 or 20 minutes for the right smooth texture and baked slowly in a moderate oven. The ideal beaten biscuit is dry all over, slightly soft in the middle, lightly browned on the bottom, and a creamy color on top. It may take a few tries to develop the right knack, but once you've perfected the art, you'll understand why certain enthusiasts believe there simply is no other biscuit. And if you're really curious about what the original American biscuit tasted like, substitute lard for the shortening. In any case, make plenty of these.

Makes about 50 biscuits

4 cups all-purpose flour
1 1/2 teaspoons salt
5 tablespoons chilled vegetable shortening
1 to 1 1/2 cups water, as needed

In the parlors of antebellum Southern plantations, beaten biscuits were routinely served with sherry or port, but, considering the effort involved in making the small biscuits, it was just as common to reserve their laborious production for occasions when special dishes had been prepared for special guests. It was said that cooks "gave the dough 200 licks for the home folks and 500 if company was expected."

1. Preheat the oven to 350°F.

2. In a large mixing bowl, combine the flour and salt and stir well. Add the shortening and rub it into the flour with your fingertips till the mixture is mealy. Gradually add enough of the water to form a soft dough, stirring with a wooden spoon.

3. Transfer the dough to a lightly floured work surface and begin beating it all over with a floured rolling pin, folding it back on itself as it flattens, and beating constantly till very smooth, at least 15 minutes.

4. Pinch off small pieces of the dough about the size of a large marble, roll between the palms of your hands, and place on a baking sheet about 1/2 inch apart. Flatten the balls with a fork, then press again to form a crisscross pattern. Bake in the upper third of the oven till the biscuits are lightly golden and quite crisp, about 30 minutes.

"[Beaten biscuits] are the most laborious of cakes, and also the most unwholesome, even when made in the best manner. . . . Children should not eat these biscuits—nor grown adults either, if they can get any other sort of bread. When living in a town where there are bakers, there is no excuse for making Maryland biscuit."

—ELIZA LESLIE, *Directions for Cookery in Its Various Branches*, 1837

Zephyrinas

I don't think I ever knew anybody (my mother included) who understood biscuits better than Bill Neal, who ran Crook's Corner restaurant in Chapel Hill, North Carolina. Bill was particularly expert at making beaten biscuits, and he always insisted that there are no short cuts, no appliances, nothing that can help with the tedious job of banging the dough repeatedly till it's smooth as velvet. Zephyrinas, a specialty of Charleston, South Carolina, and a term that refers to Zephyros, the Greek god of wind, were one of Bill's prides and joys, intended to be given as a gift to close friends.

Makes about 25 biscuits

2 cups all-purpose flour
$^1/_2$ teaspoon salt
2 tablespoons chilled lard, cut into bits
$^1/_2$ cup water

1. In a large mixing bowl, combine the flour and salt and stir well. Add the lard and rub it into the flour with your fingertips till the mixture is almost mealy. Add the water and stir till the dry ingredients are just moistened.

2. Transfer the dough to a lightly floured work surface and begin beating it with a rolling pin or hammer, folding the dough back on itself as it flattens. Continue beating till the dough is very, very smooth and almost plastic-like, at least 15 minutes.

3. Preheat the oven to 400°F.

4. Pinch off small balls of dough about the size of marbles and roll between the palms of your hands to smooth. Arrange on a baking sheet about $^1/_2$ inch apart, flatten very thin with a fork, making a crisscross pattern with the prongs, and bake in the upper third of the oven till the biscuits puff and brown lightly, about 10 minutes.

5. Transfer the biscuits with a metal spatula to a wire rack to cool and store in an airtight container up to 1 week.

Angel Biscuits

Often called "bride's biscuits" in some areas of the country since the double leavening supposedly guarantees a feather-light biscuit for even the most inexperienced cook, angel biscuits have been a popular bread in America for at least a century. At the legendary Mary Mac's Tearoom in Atlanta, the biscuits are made even lighter by substituting lard for shortening, and to achieve a slight exterior crispness from top to bottom, some Southern cooks brush the biscuits with melted butter, bake them a few minutes in the bottom of the oven, then finish them off on the middle rack. Wrapped lightly in plastic, this dough will keep about two days in the refrigerator.

Makes about 20 biscuits

1 envelope active dry yeast
$^1/_4$ cup warm water
2 $^1/_2$ cups all-purpose flour
2 tablespoons sugar
1 $^1/_2$ teaspoons baking powder
$^1/_2$ teaspoon baking soda
$^1/_2$ teaspoon salt
$^1/_2$ cup chilled vegetable shortening
1 cup buttermilk

1. In a small bowl, combine the yeast and warm water, stir, and set aside to proof.

2. In a large mixing bowl, whisk together the flour, sugar, baking powder, baking soda, and salt. Add the shortening and cut it in with a pastry cutter or rub with your fingertips till the mixture is mealy. Add the yeast mixture and buttermilk and stir with a fork just till a soft, sticky dough forms.

3. Transfer the dough to a lightly floured work surface, form into a ball, roll out $^1/_2$ inch thick, and cut out rounds with a 2-inch biscuit cutter. Roll the scraps together and cut out more rounds. Arrange the rounds close together on a baking sheet, cover with a clean kitchen towel, and let rise in a warm area about 1 hour.

4. Preheat the oven to 400°F.

5. Bake the biscuits in the center of the oven till golden brown, 12 to 15 minutes.

Sam's Cloud Biscuits

My friend Sam Segari in Houston prides himself on various dishes made with superior Gulf shrimp and crabmeat, but what people really exclaim most about are the "short," slightly sweet, and billowy cloud biscuits he turns out by the dozens for virtually any meal. One secret, of course, is the half-cup of cake flour, considerable amount of shortening, and egg; the other is the quick baking at relatively high heat.

Makes about 2 dozen biscuits

1 1/2 cups all-purpose flour
1/2 cup cake flour
1 tablespoon sugar
4 teaspoons baking powder
1/2 teaspoon salt
1/2 cup chilled vegetable shortening
2/3 cup whole milk
1 large egg, beaten

1. Preheat the oven to 475°F.

2. In a large mixing bowl, whisk together the two flours, sugar, baking powder, and salt. Add the shortening and cut it in with a pastry cutter or rub with your fingertips till the mixture is very mealy. In a glass measuring cup, whisk together the milk and egg, add to the dry mixture, and stir with a fork just till the dough follows the fork around the bowl.

3. Transfer the dough to a lightly floured work surface and knead gently 4 to 5 times. Roll out the dough about 1/4 inch thick and cut out rounds with a 2-inch biscuit cutter. Roll the scraps together and cut out more rounds.

4. Arrange the rounds fairly close together on two baking sheets. Bake in the center of the oven till just golden, 10 to 12 minutes.

biscuit bonus

When measuring solid shortening in a measuring cup, push it down into the bottom of the cup so that no space is left, thus assuring an accurate measurement. To minimize the messy procedure, wrap two fingers with part of a paper towel, then discard the towel.

Sour Milk Biscuits

Nothing (including butter-milk) makes tangier biscuits than whole milk that has soured in the refrigerator, and quite often I'll purposefully allow the last remains of a quart or half-gallon to sour and thicken when I know I'll be making these biscuits which are so perfect with soups and virtually any stew. I like them particularly thick so there'll be plenty of soft insides to sop up broth or sauce. The main point to remember is that there's at least one good reason to never again pour soured milk down the drain.

Makes 12 to 16 biscuits

2 cups all-purpose flour
2 teaspoons baking powder
1 teaspoon salt
1/2 teaspoon baking soda
4 teaspoons chilled lard or vegetable shortening
1 cup sour whole milk

1. Preheat the oven to 425°F.

2. In a large mixing bowl, whisk together the flour, baking powder, salt, and baking soda. Add the lard and cut it in with a pastry cutter till the mixture is mealy. Add the milk and stir just till a soft, sticky dough forms, adding a little more sour milk if necessary.

3. Transfer the dough to a lightly floured work surface and knead about 8 times. Pat out the dough 1/2 to 3/4 inch thick and cut out rounds with a 2-inch biscuit cutter. Pat the scraps together and cut out more rounds.

4. Arrange the rounds on a baking sheet about 1/2 inch apart and bake in the upper third of the oven till golden brown, about 15 minutes.

biscuit bonus

Commercial lard (generally available in packages around the meat department of most supermarkets) should be pure white, smooth as jelly, and not in the least rancid when sniffed. The finest is leaf lard (the fat around pigs' kidneys), often available fresh in butcher shops. Store lard in the refrigerator.

Cathead Biscuits

Since I've eaten cathead biscuits in both the Midwest and the South (where they're also called scratch biscuits in some areas), I have no idea where and how the clever name originated. One theory holds that the biscuits are as big as a cat's head; another that the irregular tops formed by hand resemble fur; and still another that the craggy ridges look like a cat's ears. Whatever the quaint explanation, real catheads must be made and shaped by hand (and never cut evenly with a biscuit cutter), the flour-and-lard mixture should be more crumbly than mealy, and the biscuits must be baked in heavy cast-iron skillets.

Makes about 1½ dozen biscuits

3 cups all-purpose flour
4 teaspoons baking powder
½ teaspoon baking soda
1 teaspoon salt
1 cup chilled lard, cut into pieces
1 cup buttermilk

1. Preheat the oven to 425°F. Grease two large cast-iron skillets and set aside.

2. In a large mixing bowl, whisk together the flour, baking powder, baking soda, and salt. Add the lard and cut it in with a pastry cutter or rub with your fingertips till the mixture is just crumbly. Gradually stir in just enough buttermilk to form a soft ball of dough.

3. Transfer the dough to a lightly floured work surface, knead about 8 times, then shape by hand into biscuits about 3½ inches across and 1 inch high.

4. Arrange the biscuits fairly close together in the prepared skillets and bake in the upper third of the oven till golden brown, about 17 minutes.

"When I think about my grandmother, I always remember arriving at her home and going to the food chest and getting a cathead biscuit. Her biscuits were good even cold. When we were lucky enough to be there when they came out of the oven, we broke them open and spread fresh churned butter on each side with homemade peach or fig preserves or cane or sorghum."

—TIM PATRIDGE, Atlanta chef, teacher, and food writer

Clabber Biscuits

C labber the residual liquid derived from semisolid sour milk, has been used throughout the American East and South to make all sorts of breads and desserts since at least the eighteenth century, and I can still remember my maternal grandmother sniffing a bottle of milk in the refrigerator and exclaiming, "Whew! I better make up a batch of biscuit!" (the word always used only in the singular) It's rare to find real clabber today but these tangy biscuits made with sour cream bear a close resemblance to the ones Maw Maw used to turn out in little more than 20 minutes. Traditionally, these biscuits are quite thin.

Makes about 2 dozen biscuits

2 1/2 cups all-purpose flour
4 teaspoons baking powder
1 teaspoon baking soda
1 teaspoon salt
1/3 cup chilled butter, cut into pieces
1 1/2 cups sour cream (don't use lowfat or nonfat)

1. Preheat the oven to 425°F.

2. In a large mixing bowl, whisk together the flour, baking powder, baking soda, and salt. Add the butter and cut it in with a pastry cutter or rub with your fingertips till the mixture is mealy. Add the sour cream and stir till the dough is soft and slightly sticky, adding a little more sour cream if necessary.

3. Transfer the dough to a lightly floured work surface and knead about 6 times. Pat out the dough 1/4 inch thick and cut out rounds with a 2- to 2 1/2-inch biscuit cutter. Pat the scraps together and cut out more rounds.

4. Arrange on one or two baking sheets about 1/2 inch apart and bake in the upper third of the oven till lightly browned on top, 13 to 15 minutes.

Shirley's Touch of Grace Biscuits

Shirley Corriher, author of *Cookwise*, is recognized by many today as the South's leading biscuit lady and, without doubt, nobody is more passionate about biscuits. Having had trouble for years reproducing her Georgia grandmother's flaky biscuits (just as I still have trouble making my mother's perfect ones), she relates how the older lady admonished, "Honey, I guess you forgot to add a touch of grace." Since I'm not crazy about any sweetened plain raised biscuit, and also feel that brushing the rounds with melted butter before baking (as Shirley does) affects the outer texture of the biscuit too much, I've modified the recipe somewhat to suit my own taste. In any case, these are no doubt some of the best hand-formed buttermilk biscuits you'll ever sample, the main secret (or "touch of grace") being the unusually wet dough, which creates more steam in the oven and hence a very light biscuit. The trick to dealing with the sticky dough is not only to sprinkle a little flour over each lump as the biscuits are formed, but to keep your hands well-floured as well. Shirley, like myself, is adamant about using only Southern self-rising flour for these biscuits but concedes that, if absolutely necessary, an acceptable substitute is 1 cup all-purpose flour, $1/2$ cup cake flour, and $1/2$ teaspoon baking powder. As for cutting instead of breaking the cooked biscuits apart, I'll let her argue with Southern purists on that touchy score.

Makes about 10 biscuits

$1^1/_2$ cups Southern self-rising flour (such as White Lily, Martha White, or Red Band)

2 teaspoons sugar

$^1/_8$ teaspoon baking soda

$^1/_3$ teaspoon salt

3 tablespoons chilled vegetable shortening

1 to $1^1/_4$ cups buttermilk, as needed

1 cup bleached all-purpose flour for shaping

biscuit bonus

For feather-light biscuits, a wet, sticky dough is best since it produces plenty of steam in the hot oven. To handle the dough, lightly flour both the dough and your hands.

1. Preheat the oven to 475°F. Grease an 8-inch round cake pan and set aside.

2. In a large mixing bowl, whisk together the self-rising flour, sugar, baking soda, and salt. Add the shortening and rub it in with your fingertips till there are no shortening lumps larger than a big pea. Add 1 cup of the buttermilk, stir lightly, add more buttermilk as necessary to form a sticky dough, and let stand 2 to 3 minutes (the dough will be very wet).

3. Pour the all-purpose flour onto a plate and flour your hands well. Spoon a biscuit-size lump of wet dough onto the flour and sprinkle flour over the dough to coat the outside. Shape the lump into a soft round with your hands, shaking off excess flour. Make more rounds till the dough is used up, arrange them tightly against each other in the prepared pan, and bake in the upper third of the oven till lightly browned, about 15 minutes. Let cool 1 or 2 minutes in the pan, then turn the biscuits out and cut them apart. Serve hot.

The original "ship's biscuit" (or "hardtack") aboard eighteenth-century fishing vessels was an unleavened flatbread made of the coarsest whole-wheat dough that was rolled flat, baked, and stored till completely dried out and hard. A "captain's biscuit" was made with more refined flour and was slightly softer.

Butter-Yogurt Biscuits

nriched cake flour milled from soft wheat is generally not recommended by itself for biscuit making since its texture is so fine. Fortify the flour with sturdy agents like butter and yogurt, however, pat out the biscuits rather thick, and bake them quickly in a hot oven and the exceptionally tender, crisp, rich results are delectable.

Makes about 1 dozen biscuits

2 cups cake flour
3 teaspoons baking powder
1 teaspoon baking soda
$1/2$ teaspoon salt
5 tablespoons chilled butter, cut into bits
1 cup plain yogurt (don't use lowfat or nonfat)

1. Preheat the oven to 475°F. Grease a baking sheet and set aside.

2. In a large mixing bowl, whisk together the flour, baking powder, baking soda, and salt. Add the butter and cut it in with a pastry cutter or rub with your fingertips till the mixture is mealy. Add the yogurt and stir till a soft ball of dough forms.

3. Transfer the dough to a lightly floured work surface and knead about 8 times. Pat out the dough about $3/4$ inch thick and cut out rounds with a 2-inch biscuit cutter. Pat the scraps together and cut out more rounds.

4. Arrange the rounds on the prepared baking sheet about $1/2$ inch apart and bake in the upper third of the oven till just golden, 10 to 12 minutes.

Old-Fashioned Stovetop Biscuits

Legend has it that these brown, slightly crunchy, incredibly flavorful biscuits hail back to the days when everything in a farmhouse was cooked on top of a stove during the winter to save as much precious heating wood as possible. If fried correctly, the biscuits should be crusty brown on the outside and slightly soft inside. The heat of the fat is right when a morsel of dough dropped in it begins to sizzle.

Makes about 1 dozen biscuits

2 cups all-purpose flour
4 teaspoons baking powder
1 teaspoon salt
¼ cup chilled lard, cut into bits
1 cup whole milk
¼ cup lard for frying

1. In a large mixing bowl, whisk together the flour, baking powder, and salt. Add the chilled lard and cut it in with a pastry cutter or rub with your fingertips till the mixture is mealy. Add the milk and mix till the dough is smooth. Pinch off 12 pieces of dough of equal size, form each piece into a ball, and flatten the balls with your hands to about ¼ inch thick.

2. In a medium-size cast-iron skillet, melt 2 tablespoons of the lard over medium-low heat, add half the flattened balls, fry till both sides of the biscuits are browned, about 12 minutes in all, and drain on paper towels. Repeat with the remaining 2 tablespoons lard and the remaining dough balls. Serve hot.

biscuit bonus

Contrary to what most people are led to believe, 1 tablespoon of lard contains 12 mg. of cholesterol versus 33 mg. in the same quantity of butter.

Ranch Fried Soda Biscuits

During the early days of westward expansion in America, pioneers and settlers might still not have had baking powder (introduced in 1856) to leaven their biscuits but at least they could take advantage of a product sold in a bright red package called saleratus (i.e., baking soda). Flour, buttermilk, and lard were fairly plentiful, but since most food had to be cooked over open fires, biscuits were simply fried quickly in deep, cast-iron pots. Fried soda biscuits are still popular at rural cook-outs throughout Texas and other Western states, one reason being that they go so well with barbe-cued meats and chili. Be sure to fry these biscuits just till they are golden and puffy—no longer.

Makes about 2 dozen small biscuits

2 1/2 **cups all-purpose flour**
2 **teaspoons baking soda**
1 1/2 **teaspoons salt**
1/4 **cup chilled lard, cut into small pieces**
1 1/4 **cups buttermilk**
Tabasco sauce to taste
Vegetable oil for deep-frying

1. In a large mixing bowl, whisk together the flour, baking soda, and salt. Add the lard and cut it in with a pastry cutter or rub with your fingertips till the mixture is mealy. Gradually add the buttermilk, stirring just till the dough is soft and adding the Tabasco while stirring.

2. Transfer the dough to a lightly floured work surface, knead about 8 times, roll out 1/2 inch thick, and cut out rounds with a 1 1/2-inch biscuit cutter. Roll the scraps together and cut out more rounds.

3. In a large, deep cast-iron skillet, heat about 1 inch of oil to 350°F, when a speck of dough tossed in sputters. Add the biscuits in batches, cover the skillet, and fry for 4 minutes. Turn the biscuits over with a slotted spoon, cover, and fry till golden and puffy, about 4 minutes longer. Drain on paper towels and keep hot.

Yankee Rye Biscuits

Since rye flourishes in cool climates and poor soil, these sturdy, buttery, slightly sweet biscuits have been staples throughout New England ever since the region's first settlers. Rye flour by itself, however, tends to yield heavy breads, so regional cooks learned a long time ago to leaven their biscuits not only with plenty of baking powder and a little baking soda but also with wheat flour. Nothing goes better with full-flavored soups, stews, and roasts than these fairly large, hearty biscuits baked till lightly browned on top.

Makes at least 1 dozen biscuits

1 1/2 **cups rye flour**
1 1/2 **cups all-purpose flour**
4 **teaspoons baking powder**
1/2 **teaspoon baking soda**
1 **teaspoon sugar**
1 **teaspoon salt**
6 **tablespoons (3/4 stick) chilled butter, cut into bits**
1 1/2 **cups whole milk**

1. Preheat the oven to 425°F. Grease a baking sheet and set aside.

2. In a large mixing bowl, whisk together the flours, baking powder, baking soda, sugar, and salt. Add the butter and cut it in with a pastry cutter till the mixture is mealy. Add the milk and stir just till the dough is soft and still sticky.

3. Transfer the dough to a lightly floured work surface, knead 4 to 5 times, roll out 1/2 inch thick, and cut out rounds with a 3-inch biscuit cutter. Roll the scraps together and cut out more rounds.

4. Arrange the rounds on the prepared baking sheet and bake in the center of the oven till light brown, about 15 minutes.

Missouri Bran Biscuits

I was first exposed to bran biscuits while living in Missouri, and possibly the best I ever tasted were baked by a close friend's mother up in St. Joseph each and every time she served one of her chicken and vegetable stews. The biscuits are slightly coarse, and since I relish the sturdy texture when eating stick-to-the-ribs food, I sometimes even substitute cracked wheat for the bran. Whichever grain you use, be sure to soak it in milk a few minutes before adding to the flour.

Makes about 16 biscuits

2 cups all-purpose flour
1 tablespoon baking powder
1 teaspoon salt
6 tablespoons ($3/4$ stick) chilled butter, cut into bits
$1/2$ cup wheat bran
1 cup whole milk

1. Preheat the oven to 425°F. Grease a baking sheet and set aside.

2. In a large mixing bowl, whisk together the flour, baking powder, and salt. Add the butter and cut it in with a pastry cutter till the mixture is mealy. In a small mixing bowl, combine the bran and milk and let stand for 2 minutes, then add to the flour mixture and stir till a soft dough forms.

3. Transfer the dough to a lightly floured work surface, knead 3 to 4 times, roll out the dough $1/2$ inch thick, and cut out rounds with a 2-inch biscuit cutter. Roll the scraps together and cut out more rounds.

4. Arrange the rounds on the prepared baking sheet and bake in the center of the oven till golden brown, about 15 minutes.

Indian Cornmeal Biscuits

American Indians have been baking (or frying) rough, crunchy, uneven cornmeal biscuits for centuries, and while those made traditionally with only cornmeal, lard, and water can be heavy and unappetizing, once they're leavened with wheat flour, a little baking soda, and eggs and softened with a little milk, the biscuits are truly special.

Makes about 1 dozen biscuits

1 cup yellow cornmeal
1 cup all-purpose flour
1 teaspoon salt
$^1/_2$ teaspoon baking soda
$^1/_4$ cup chilled lard, cut into small pieces
2 large eggs, beaten
$^2/_3$ cup whole milk

1. Preheat the oven to 425°F.

2. In a large mixing bowl, combine the cornmeal, flour, salt, and baking soda, whisking them quickly together with your fingers. Add the lard and rub it in with your fingertips till the mixture is mealy. Add the eggs and milk and stir till the dough is firm, adding a little more cornmeal if necessary. (You don't want a very sticky dough.)

3. Transfer the dough to a lightly floured work surface and knead with your fingertips about 15 seconds. Divide the dough into 12 pieces and pat each into a disk about $^3/_4$ inch thick and $1^1/_2$ inches in diameter.

4. Arrange the disks on a baking sheet and bake in the center of the oven till puffy and golden brown, about 15 minutes.

biscuit bonus

To make your own lard, slowly melt any white pork fat in a heavy saucepan, strain it into a bowl, let cool completely, and store tightly covered in the refrigerator up to one month.

Jewish Yeast Biscuits

Like so many breads in classic Jewish cookery (kulich, stollen, bannocks, and various buns and rolls), the yeast for these biscuits is not proofed but added directly to the dry ingredients. Nor is the shortening cut or rubbed in but heated with the other liquids and beaten with the dry ingredients with an electric mixer to form a fairly thick but soft dough. The overall procedure is totally unorthodox in traditional biscuit making, but the result is beautifully leavened biscuits that are nicely browned on the outside and fluffy inside. Remember that this dough, unlike that for most other biscuits, should not be very sticky.

Makes about 20 biscuits

2 to $2^1/2$ cups all-purpose flour, as needed
1 teaspoon salt
$1^1/2$ tablespoons sugar
1 teaspoon baking powder
1 envelope active dry yeast
$^1/2$ cup whole milk
$^1/2$ cup water
$^1/2$ cup chilled vegetable shortening

1. In a large mixing bowl, combine $1^1/2$ cups of the flour, the salt, sugar, baking powder, and yeast and whisk till well blended.

2. In a small saucepan, combine the milk, water, and shortening over medium heat and heat just till the shortening begins to melt. Gradually add the liquid mixture to the dry ingredients and beat with an electric mixer till the dough is soft. Add $^1/2$ cup more flour and beat till the dough thickens. Scrape the sides of the bowl down with a wooden spoon, then add enough additional flour to make a very soft, smooth dough.

3. Scrape the dough onto a lightly floured work surface and knead till a very smooth, round ball forms, about 1 minute. Roll out the dough $^1/2$ inch thick and cut out rounds with a 2-inch biscuit cutter. Roll the scraps together and cut out more rounds.

4. Arrange the rounds on a baking sheet about $^1/2$ inch apart, cover with a dish towel, and let rise in a warm area till almost doubled in height, about 1 hour.

5. Preheat the oven to 400°F. Bake the biscuits in the upper third of the oven till golden brown, 15 to 20 minutes. Serve hot.

Biscuit Muffins

Biscuit muffins are a specialty in Mississippi, Louisiana, and other states in the Deep South, brown, crusty little dodgers that are not only spread with homemade fruit preserves for breakfast but relished at social teas and even cocktail parties. Unlike most Southern biscuits, these are always slightly sweet, and do notice that they require lengthy baking at a moderate temperature for just the right texture.

Makes 1 dozen muffins

2 1/2 cups bleached all-purpose flour
2 tablespoons sugar
2 teaspoons baking powder
1 teaspoon salt
1/4 teaspoon baking soda
10 tablespoons (1 1/4 sticks) chilled butter, cut into bits
1 cup buttermilk

1. Preheat the oven to 350°F. Grease a muffin tin with 12 cups (each about 1/3-cup capacity) and set aside.

2. In a large mixing bowl, whisk together the flour, sugar, baking powder, salt, and baking soda. Add the butter and rub it into the flour with your fingertips till the mixture is mealy. Add the buttermilk and stir till the dough is slightly firm.

3. Spoon the mixture into the prepared muffin tin and bake in the center of the oven till brown and crusty, 40 to 45 minutes, checking carefully to make sure they don't overbrown.

biscuit bonus

If an acidic liquid (buttermilk, yogurt, vinegar, molasses, honey, fruit juice, etc.) is used to make biscuits, be sure to add a little baking soda to the dough.

Buttermilk Biscuit Yeast Rolls

Because of the yeast, no baking powder is needed to make these buttery rolls light and fluffy. If you prefer a flakier roll, use less chilled butter and more lard, but, in either case, don't fail to brush them with melted butter to ensure rich, beautifully browned tops.

Makes about 1½ dozen rolls

2 cups all-purpose flour

2 teaspoons sugar

½ teaspoon salt

¼ teaspoon baking soda

2 tablespoons chilled butter, cut into bits

1 tablespoon chilled lard, cut into bits

1 envelope active dry yeast

3 tablespoons warm water

½ cup buttermilk

2 tablespoons butter, or more to taste, melted

1. In a large mixing bowl, whisk together the flour, sugar, salt, and baking soda. Add the chilled butter and lard and rub them into the flour with your fingertips till the mixture is mealy. In a small bowl, sprinkle the yeast over the water and stir to dissolve. Add the buttermilk and stir till well blended, then pour into the dry mixture and stir just till a soft dough forms.

2. Transfer the dough to a lightly floured work surface and knead till elastic, about 5 minutes. Form the dough into a ball, place in a buttered bowl, cover with plastic wrap, and let rise in a warm area till doubled in bulk, about 1 hour.

3. Grease a baking sheet. Punch the dough down, transfer to a lightly floured work surface, and knead for about 1 minute. Form the dough into ovals about 1½ inches in diameter, arrange on the prepared baking sheet about 1½ inches apart, cover, and let rise again till doubled in bulk, about 30 minutes.

4. Preheat the oven to 425°F. Brush the rolls with the melted butter and bake in the center of the oven till nicely browned, about 20 minutes.

Olive Oil Biscuits

Damon Lee Fowler is probably the most talented and respected cooking teacher and food writer in Savannah, Georgia, but when he told me about these unorthodox biscuits he'd created for his lowfat-obsessed mother, I thought he'd lost his mind. Olive oil in place of shortening, lard, or butter; no baking soda to neutralize the buttermilk; folding the biscuit dough over itself repeatedly; a 500°F oven—he'd broken every rule imaginable in traditional Southern biscuit making. Then I tested the technique, and while I still miss the short, tender, flaky texture produced by standard fats and minimum handling of the dough, I have to admit there's something intriguing and delectable about these smooth, almost silky biscuits made with olive oil. Of course, Fowler uses only soft-wheat Southern flour (as I usually do), but if that's impractical, the flour combination I've indicated works almost as well.

Makes about 16 biscuits

1 cup all-purpose flour

1 cup cake flour

2 teaspoons baking powder

1 teaspoon salt

2 tablespoons extra-virgin olive oil

$3/4$ cup buttermilk, or plain yogurt diluted with whole milk to a buttermilk consistency

1. Preheat the oven to 500°F.

2. In a large mixing bowl, whisk together both flours, the baking powder, and salt. In a small mixing bowl, combine the olive oil with $2/3$ cup of the buttermilk and stir till well blended.

3. Make a well in the center of the flour mixture, add the olive oil mixture, and stir till the dough clumps together and pulls away from the sides of the bowl. Add the remaining buttermilk and stir till the dough is no longer crumbly. Transfer the dough to a lightly floured work surface, pat out $1/2$ inch thick, fold in half, and pat out again. Repeat folding and patting 5 or 6 times, then pat out $1/2$ inch thick. Cut out rounds with a 2-inch biscuit cutter and arrange on a baking sheet about $1/2$ inch apart. Gather up the scraps, fold the dough over itself 3 times, pat out $1/2$ inch thick, and cut out more rounds. Bake in the center of the oven till the biscuits are golden brown, about 10 minutes.

Chuck-Wagon Sourdough Biscuits

To us today, it seems almost inconceivable how, during western expansion in the nineteenth century, chuck-wagon cooks and cowboys could turn out scores of sourdough biscuits in the bottom of Dutch ovens over open fires. Traditionally, a sourdough starter of flour, warm water, and maybe a little sugar was begun in a crock or large keg and allowed to ferment over a number of days as yeast organisms in the air and bacteria in the flour interacted to create a tangy batter. When added to fresh dough, the fermented batter would both leaven and flavor the biscuits, the trick being to keep the starter going indefinitely by replacing the used batter with equal amounts of flour and water. Like today, it was an unpredictable, often frustrating process dependent on the type of flour, the right blend of natural yeasts and bacteria, and even the temperature and humidity in a given locale. Though it certainly helps now to have active dry yeast to boost the starter, sourdough biscuits can still present a touchy challenge even with our more sophisticated equipment and baking techniques. The biscuits, however, relate to an important chapter in our history and are actually quite simple and fun to make (not to mention utterly delicious) once you deal successfully with the starter. Just remember that these biscuits do tend to burn on the bottom more easily than regular ones.

Makes 12 to 16 biscuits

Sourdough Starter:
2 cups warm water
1 envelope active dry yeast
1 tablespoon sugar
2 cups all-purpose flour

Biscuits:
2 cups all-purpose flour
2 teaspoons baking powder
1 teaspoon baking soda
1 teaspoon salt
1/2 cup chilled lard, cut into pieces
1 1/2 cups sourdough starter

In the South, riz biscuits refer to any biscuit that contains yeast. Riz (or riz'd) biscuits are the same as angel and bride's biscuits.

1. To make the starter, combine the water, yeast, and sugar in a large glass or ceramic mixing bowl, stir, and let stand till slightly bubbly. Add the flour and stir till the batter is well blended and almost runny. Cover the bowl with a clean towel or plastic wrap and let stand in a warm area at least 2 or 3 days, stirring several times a day. (The batter should develop a pungent sour smell and remain liquidy.) To keep the starter going indefinitely, replace the amount used for biscuits with equal amounts of warm water and flour, stir well, and store in a large, tightly sealed jar in the refrigerator till ready to return to room temperature and use again.

2. Grease a baking sheet well.

3. To make the biscuits, in a large mixing bowl, whisk together the flour, baking powder, baking soda, and salt. Add the lard and rub it in with your fingertips till the mixture is mealy. Add the starter and stir till the dough is just sticky. Transfer to a lightly floured work surface and knead lightly 4 or 5 times. Pinch off medium-size balls of dough and, with floured hands, pat into smooth rounds about 1/2 inch thick till all the dough is used up. Arrange the rounds on the prepared baking sheet about 1/2 inch apart, cover with a towel, and let rest about 30 minutes.

4. Preheat the oven to 425°F. Bake the biscuits in the upper third of the oven till golden brown, 12 to 15 minutes, watching carefully to make sure they don't burn on the bottom.

"[In the old days], sourdough biscuits were standard breakfast bread on farms and ranches, where chores were done before the morning meal. On cattle drives, where nights were apt to be chilly, the cook-wagon 'chef' usually mixed the dough the night before and set the biscuits in a reflector oven or frying pan to be cooked the next morning."

—JAMES BEARD, *American Cookery*, 1980

Flavored Biscuits

From all historical indications, American biscuits flavored with ingredients other than salt and perhaps soured milk virtually did not exist before the middle of the nineteenth century, and even Fannie Farmer, in *The Boston Cooking-School Cook Book* of 1896, limited her biscuits pretty much to the basic formula of flour, baking powder, fat, and milk. No doubt pioneers and settlers during western expansion were adding a few pork cracklings to their open-fire biscuits and I suspect that around the time of the Civil War, Southern cooks were probably already enhancing their clabber biscuits with bits of cured ham, molasses, and various seeds and nuts. But for all intents and purposes, the flavored biscuit is a twentieth-century innovation that not only expanded the whole process of biscuit making but added a new dimension to our overall gastronomy that continues to evolve.

It seems that the first major ingredient used to transform ordinary baking powder biscuits into a more versatile bread was cheese, followed by various pureed vegetables and fruits, minced meats and seafood, herbs and condiments, and crushed nuts. The recipes in this chapter serve only as an enticing starting point to the dozens of possibilities that exist today with our bounty of new and interesting ingredients: exotic goat cheeses and mushrooms, different mustards and seasonings, multiple varieties of herbs and olives, and all sorts of fascinating dried fruits and sweetening agents. As many of these recipes demonstrate, the world of flavored biscuits is open to imaginative cooks everywhere, and so long as we take the precaution of never compromising the integrity of the biscuit itself, there's really no limit to what we can create.

Cheddar Biscuits

Cheese biscuits seem to have been an all-American twentieth-century innovation and today the styles vary enormously from region to region. Because of all the cheese and butter, these cheddar biscuits are not intended to be fluffy, but the flavor is incomparable. Just be sure to use extra-sharp cheddar, and by no means handle this dough too much. For even more intense cheese flavor, I often reduce the amount of cheddar slightly and add a little freshly grated genuine Parmesan—or simply use equal amounts of cheddar and Parmesan. (Experiment also with other cheeses: goat, Monterey Jack, blue, feta, etc.) Note that this biscuit dough makes an interesting topping for pot pies that contain rather bland fillings.

Makes at least 1 dozen biscuits

2 cups all-purpose flour
2 teaspoons baking powder
$1/2$ teaspoon salt
6 tablespoons ($3/4$ stick) chilled butter or margarine, cut into pieces
1 cup finely grated extra-sharp cheddar cheese
Cayenne pepper to taste
1 cup milk

1. Preheat the oven to 425°F.

2. In a large mixing bowl, whisk together the flour, baking powder, and salt. Add the butter and cut it in with a pastry cutter till the mixture is mealy. Add the cheese and cayenne and stir till well blended. Add the milk and stir till the dough is soft, adding a touch more milk if necessary.

3. Transfer the dough to a lightly floured work surface and knead 3 or 4 times. Pat out the dough $1/2$ inch thick, and cut out rounds with a $2^1/2$-inch biscuit cutter. Pat the scraps together and cut out more rounds.

4. Arrange the rounds on an ungreased baking sheet about $1/2$ inch apart and bake in the upper third of the oven till golden, 12 to 13 minutes. Serve hot or at room temperature.

Spicy Sesame Cheese Biscuits

These are the spicy cheese biscuits that a hostess in Savannah, Georgia, served at a luncheon when I was in town to judge a March of Dimes Gourmet Gala. The sesame seeds really do add a nice regional touch, but the real surprise were the bits of pimento blended into the dough. Since the biscuits should be browned on all sides, be sure to bake them about 1 inch apart. I also like to serve these with cocktails.

Makes about 50 biscuits

3 cups all-purpose flour
5 teaspoons baking powder
1¹/₂ teaspoons salt
¹/₂ teaspoon cayenne pepper
¹/₂ cup chilled vegetable shortening
1 cup grated extra-sharp cheddar cheese
¹/₄ cup finely chopped pimentos
1¹/₂ cups whole milk
3 tablespoons butter, melted
Sesame seeds for topping

1. Preheat the oven to 450°F. Grease two baking sheets and set aside.

2. In a large mixing bowl, whisk together the flour, baking powder, salt, and cayenne. Add the shortening and cut it in with a pastry cutter till the mixture is mealy. Add the cheese and pimentos and stir till well blended. Add the milk and stir till the dough is soft.

3. Transfer the dough to a lightly floured work surface, form into a ball, and roll out ¹/₂ inch thick. Fold the dough in half, roll out again ¹/₂ inch thick, and cut out rounds with a 1¹/₂-inch biscuit cutter. Roll the scraps together and cut out more rounds.

4. Arrange the rounds on the prepared baking sheets about 1 inch apart. Brush the rounds with the melted butter, sprinkle sesame seeds over the tops, and bake in the upper third of the oven till nicely browned all over, about 12 minutes.

biscuit bonus

Lightly flour the rolling pin or your hands when rolling or patting out biscuit dough. Also flour the biscuit cutter before cutting out rounds.

Tomato-Parmesan Biscuits

Tomato-Parmesan-oregano is one of the classic flavor combinations in Italian-American cooking, so why not exploit it as much in biscuit making as in pastas, pizzas, and scaloppine? Although the whole wheat flour gives this biscuit a nice sturdiness, it needs to be tempered by plenty of baking powder, and to neutralize the acid of the tomato juice, baking soda is needed. Note also that the amount of fat (which is melted before being added to the dry ingredients) is considerably less than in most biscuits. I like to serve these with seafood salads and a crisp white wine.

Makes about 16 biscuits

1 cup all-purpose flour
1 cup whole wheat flour
4 teaspoons baking powder
$^1/_2$ teaspoon baking soda
1 teaspoon salt
$^1/_4$ cup freshly grated genuine Parmesan cheese
$^1/_2$ teaspoon dried oregano, finely crumbled
1 cup tomato juice
$^1/_4$ cup ($^1/_2$ stick) butter, melted and cooled

1. Preheat the oven to 425°F.

2. In a large mixing bowl, whisk together both flours, the baking powder, baking soda, and salt. Add the cheese and oregano and stir till well blended. Add the tomato juice and butter and stir till the dough is just soft but still slightly sticky.

3. Transfer to a lightly floured work surface and knead about 8 times. Pat out $^1/_2$ inch thick and cut out rounds with a 2-inch biscuit cutter. Pat the scraps together and cut out more rounds.

4. Arrange the rounds on a large baking sheet about 1 inch apart and bake in the upper third of the oven till golden brown, about 15 minutes.

Hay Day Herbed Parmesan Layered Biscuits

One of the most amazing country markets in America is the Hay Day farm stand in Westport, Connecticut, and one of the most amazing breads are the layered biscuits baked fresh daily there. The technique of folding the dough to suspend the butter and shortening in layers is not unlike the method the French use to make flaky, feather-light puff pastry, and while it is a bit time-consuming, the biscuits are nothing less than celestial. If you plan to serve this style of biscuit for breakfast, you might prefer to leave out the herbs.

Makes about 16 biscuits

2 cups all-purpose flour
1 tablespoon baking powder
1/2 teaspoon salt
1/4 cup (1/2 stick) chilled butter, cut into chunks
2 tablespoons chilled vegetable shortening, cut into chunks
1/2 cup freshly grated genuine Parmesan cheese
1/2 teaspoon dried thyme, crumbled
1/4 teaspoon dried marjoram, crumbled
1/4 teaspoon dried sage, crumbled
1/4 teaspoon black pepper
1 cup whole milk
1/4 cup white cornmeal for dusting
1 tablespoon butter, melted

1. Preheat the oven to 425°F.

2. In a food processor, combine the flour, baking powder, salt, butter, and shortening and pulse till the bits are like small grains of rice. Transfer to a large mixing bowl, add the cheese, herbs, and pepper, and stir till well blended. Gradually add the milk, stirring till the dry ingredients are just moistened.

biscuit bonus

For fluffy biscuits, always use a sharp metal biscuit cutter. A blunt one such as a juice glass tends to seal the edges of the biscuit and impede the rising action of the baking powder. Also, to avoid the same problem, always cut straight down and never twist the biscuit cutter.

3. Transfer the dough to a work surface sprinkled with the cornmeal and roll out into a rectangle $1/2$ inch thick. Fold the short ends to meet in the middle, then fold it in half at the seam to form four layers. Roll out again $1/2$ inch thick, then cut out rounds with a 2-inch biscuit cutter. Roll the scraps together and cut out more rounds.

4. Arrange the rounds on a baking sheet about 1 inch apart, brush the tops with the melted butter, and bake in the center of the oven till golden brown, about 15 minutes.

Some years before the American Civil War, biscuit makers were introduced to a new leavening called saleratus, later to be called baking soda. Although it was convenient to use, it required the help of an acid to activate its power—usually cream of tartar. When baking powder was devised in 1856, this provided the necessary acid for the baking soda.

Sweet Potato Biscuits

Once almost indigenous to the South, biscuits made with sweet potatoes or yams are now popular throughout the country, and the recipes vary dramatically, with different leavenings, seasonings, and techniques. Basically, all sweet potato biscuits tend to be heavy, so never add butter or thick liquids, don't handle the dough much, and apply as light a touch as possible when rolling out the dough. Do feel free to experiment discreetly with other spices like allspice and cinnamon. These biscuits are really not suitable for breakfast and go best with soups and stews.

Makes about 20 biscuits

5 medium-size sweet potatoes
1 cup chilled vegetable shortening
2 1/2 cups all-purpose flour
1 tablespoon baking powder
1/2 teaspoon ground nutmeg
1/2 teaspoon salt
Whole milk as needed

1. Place the potatoes in a large pot with enough water to cover, bring to a moderate simmer, cover, and cook till the potatoes are very tender, about 30 minutes. When cool enough to handle, peel the potatoes, place them in a large mixing bowl, and mash with a potato masher or heavy fork till smooth. Immediately add the shortening, continue to mash till well blended, and let cool.

2. Preheat the oven to 425°F.

3. Add the flour, baking powder, nutmeg, and salt to the potato mixture and mix till well blended, adding a little milk as necessary to make a smooth dough.

4. Transfer the dough to a lightly floured work surface, roll out 1/2 inch thick, and cut out rounds with a 2-inch biscuit cutter. Roll the scraps together and cut out more rounds.

5. Arrange the rounds on a baking sheet about 1 inch apart, and bake in the center of the oven till golden, 12 to 15 minutes.

Thomas Jefferson's Sweet Potato Biscuits

Opened in 1774, City Tavern in Philadelphia has always been a veritable repository of authentic American dishes, one of the most important being these thick, spicy, sumptuous sweet potato biscuits adapted from Thomas Jefferson's diaries and still served every day at the Tavern. Jefferson was the first true American gastronome, and while I'm sure the original biscuits baked by his cook at Monticello were leavened with little more than sodium bicarbonate or a few hundred whacks of the axe, this modernized version (which I've modified even further) gives some idea of how delicious the flavor must have been. Notice that these biscuits are baked at a relatively low temperature up to 30 minutes, just as they would have been in Jefferson's day. And, incidentally, three of Jefferson's pecan trees, dating back over 200 years, still grow at Monticello.

Makes about 1 dozen biscuits

2 1/2 cups all-purpose flour
1/2 cup firmly packed light brown sugar
1 tablespoon baking powder
1/2 teaspoon ground cinnamon
1/2 teaspoon ground ginger
1/2 teaspoon ground allspice
1/2 teaspoon salt
1/2 cup chilled lard, cut into pieces
1 cup cooked, peeled, mashed, and cooled sweet potato
1/2 cup heavy cream
1/4 cup coarsely chopped pecans

1. Preheat the oven to 350°F. Grease a baking sheet and set aside.

2. In a large mixing bowl, whisk together the flour, brown sugar, baking powder, spices, and salt. Add the lard and cut it in with a pastry cutter till the mixture is crumbly. Add the sweet potato and stir till well blended. Add the cream and pecans and stir till the dough is just moist.

3. Transfer to a lightly floured work surface, roll out 1 1/2 inches thick, and cut out rounds with a 2-inch biscuit cutter. Roll the scraps together and cut out more rounds.

4. Arrange the rounds on the prepared baking sheet about 1 inch apart and bake in the center of the oven till golden brown, 25 to 30 minutes. Serve warm or let cool on a wire rack.

Redneck Biscuits

At many barbecue joints and cafés throughout the South, ask about the hefty biscuits being served and the waitress is just as likely as not to snicker and say, "Oh, honey, these are just good old redneck biscuits." Actually, the biscuits originally came about as a way to use up a mess of leftover grits and country ham, and to make them as light and flaky as possible, the preferred fat was always lard. You talk about something good to serve with scrambled eggs and fresh fruit for breakfast! This is one biscuit dough you don't have to pamper too much.

Makes 18 to 20 biscuits

1³/₄ cups all-purpose flour
3¹/₂ teaspoons baking powder
¹/₂ teaspoon salt
3 tablespoons chilled lard
¹/₂ cup whole milk, or as needed
¹/₂ cup plain grits (not instant), cooked according to package directions and cooled
¹/₄ cup finely diced cured country ham

1. Preheat the oven to 400°F.

2. In a large mixing bowl, whisk together the flour, baking powder, and salt. Add the lard and rub it in with your fingertips till the mixture is mealy. Stir in the milk, then beat in the grits and ham with a wooden spoon till well blended, adding more milk if necessary for a smooth dough.

3. Transfer the dough to a slightly floured work surface and knead 3 to 4 times. Pat out ¹/₂ inch thick and cut out rounds with a 2-inch biscuit cutter. Pat the scraps together and cut out more rounds.

4. Arrange the rounds on a baking sheet about 1 inch apart and bake in the upper third of the oven till golden brown, about 12 minutes, checking to make sure the bottoms don't overbrown. Serve hot.

Farmhouse Crackling Biscuits

Cracklings, which are small pieces of salt pork rendered in a frying pan till very crisp, have been used to flavor breads and other foods ever since chuck-wagon days and the establishment of the nation's first farming communities. The earliest crackling biscuits were no doubt pretty heavy, but after commercial yeast was introduced in 1868, cooks were at considerably more liberty to experiment with different flours and flavoring ingredients. These biscuits are also delicious made with bits of fried bacon or country ham.

Makes about 1 dozen biscuits

1/2 envelope active dry yeast
2 tablespoons warm water
1/4 cup finely diced salt pork
2 1/4 cups unbleached all-purpose flour
1 teaspoon baking powder
1/4 cup chilled vegetable shortening
1 cup whole milk

1. In a small bowl, sprinkle the yeast over the water and set aside to proof. (If the mixture does not foam up after a few minutes, it means the yeast is no longer active and the mixture should be discarded.)

2. In a small, heavy skillet, fry the salt pork over moderate heat till well browned and crisp, about 10 minutes, then drain the cracklings on paper towels.

3. In a large mixing bowl, whisk together the flour and baking powder. Add the shortening and rub it into the flour with your fingertips till the mixture is mealy. Add the cracklings and stir till well blended. Make a well in the dry ingredients, pour the yeast mixture and milk into the well, and stir gently just till the dry ingredients are moistened and the dough is soft. Cover with plastic wrap or a clean dish towel and let rise in a warm area about 1 hour.

4. Preheat the oven to 425°F.

5. Transfer the dough to a lightly floured work surface and knead about 8 times. Roll out about 1/2 inch thick and cut out rounds with a 2 1/2-inch biscuit cutter. Roll the scraps together and cut out more rounds.

6. Arrange the rounds on a baking sheet about 1 inch apart, and bake in the upper third of the oven till golden brown, about 15 minutes.

Carolina Hominy Ham Biscuits

When Bill Neal was alive, his restaurant in Chapel Hill, North Carolina, Crook's Corner, drew people from all over the country eager to sample his authentic Southern cookery. Bill prided himself most on his biscuits, and surely none was so sumptuous as his upscale, slightly sweet rendition of "redneck biscuits" made with hominy and North Carolina's finest mountain-cured country ham. Dried hominy is available in some fine food shops (especially in the South), but since it can be a mess to deal with, I strongly recommend you use the canned variety, which can be found in most supermarkets.

Makes about 20 biscuits

1 1/2 cups all-purpose flour
2 1/2 teaspoons baking powder
1/2 teaspoon salt
1/2 teaspoon sugar
2 tablespoons chilled lard
6 tablespoons whole milk
1/2 cup canned white hominy, rinsed in a colander
1/4 cup finely diced cured country ham

1. Preheat the oven to 400°F.

2. In a large mixing bowl, whisk together the flour, baking powder, salt, and sugar. Add the lard and rub it in with your fingertips till the mixture is mealy. Stir in the milk, then beat in the hominy and ham till well blended, adding a little more milk if necessary for a soft dough.

3. Transfer the dough to a lightly floured work surface and knead 3 to 4 times. Roll out 1/2 inch thick and cut out rounds with a 1 1/2-inch biscuit cutter. Roll the scraps together and cut out more rounds.

4. Arrange the rounds on a baking sheet about 1 inch apart, and bake in the upper third of the oven till golden, about 12 minutes. Serve hot.

Sausage and Cheese Breakfast Biscuits

Both Southerners and Midwesterners love this type of composed, rugged biscuit for breakfast. The biscuits might not be the prettiest in the world, but served with creamy scrambled eggs or plain omelettes and fresh fruit, their flavor is unforgettable. I like these biscuits well seasoned, but do adjust the red pepper flakes to your own taste. If you don't have self-rising flour, simply whisk 4 teaspoons baking powder and 1 teaspoon salt into 2 cups bleached all-purpose flour.

Makes 1 dozen biscuits

$1/4$ **pound bulk pork sausage**
2 cups self-rising flour
$1/4$ **cup chilled vegetable shortening**
$1/3$ **cup grated sharp cheddar cheese**
$1/4$ **teaspoon red pepper flakes**
1 cup whole milk

1. In a medium-size, heavy skillet over medium-high heat, break up the sausage finely, fry till fully cooked, stirring, remove from the pan with a slotted spoon, and drain on paper towels to cool.

2. Preheat the oven to 425°F. Grease a large baking sheet and set aside.

3. In a large mixing bowl, combine the flour and shortening, rubbing them together with your fingertips till the mixture is mealy. Add the sausage, cheese, and red pepper flakes and stir till well blended. Add the milk and stir till a soft, slightly sticky dough forms.

4. Transfer the dough to a lightly floured work surface and knead about 8 times. With your hands lightly floured, form the dough into 12 ovals about $1/2$ inch thick, arrange on the prepared baking sheet about $1^1/2$ inches apart, and bake in the center of the oven till the biscuits are golden, about 15 minutes. Serve hot.

biscuit bonus

When using self-rising flour for biscuits, remember to omit any baking powder and salt unless additional amounts are desired.

Olive-Pimento Cream Biscuits

In California and Oregon, these creamy biscuits are usually made with chopped roasted red bell peppers and black olives, but if you don't want to go to the trouble of roasting peppers and pitting olives (and I usually don't), you'll find that pimento-stuffed green olives provide a delightfully salty foil to the rich butter and cream. These biscuits are delicious with virtually all soups and any simple composed salad.

Makes about 16 biscuits

2 cups all-purpose flour
1 tablespoon baking powder
$^1/_2$ teaspoon salt
$^1/_4$ teaspoon sugar
6 tablespoons ($^3/_4$ stick) chilled butter, cut into bits
$^3/_4$ cup half-and-half
$^1/_2$ cup finely chopped pimento-stuffed green olives

1. Preheat the oven to 425°F. Grease a baking sheet and set aside.

2. In a large mixing bowl, whisk together the flour, baking powder, salt, and sugar. Add the butter and rub it into the flour with your fingertips till the mixture is mealy. Add the half-and-half and olives and stir till the dough is well blended but still slightly sticky, adding more half-and-half if necessary.

3. Transfer the dough to a lightly floured work surface and knead about 8 times. Pat out about $^1/_2$ inch thick and cut out rounds with a 2-inch biscuit cutter. Pat the scraps together and cut out more rounds.

4. Arrange the rounds on the prepared baking sheet about 1 inch apart, and bake in the center of the oven till golden brown, about 15 minutes.

Onion–Poppy Seed Biscuits

Silver-blue, nutty-tasting poppy seeds make an interesting component not only in all sorts of pastries, salads, cakes, and rice and noodle dishes but also in biscuits like these small, rather fancy ones leavened with both baking powder and beaten eggs. I like to pass a tray of the biscuits at any simple lunch featuring cold meats or a composed seafood or chicken salad. These are also delectable snack biscuits, as well as a last-minute treat for cocktail parties. Think about doubling the recipe and storing the biscuits in an airtight container for emergencies. Mine keep well at least two weeks.

Makes about 25 biscuits

2 cups all-purpose flour
1 tablespoon baking powder
1 teaspoon salt
Black pepper to taste
¹/₄ cup chilled vegetable shortening
1 large onion, minced
¹/₄ cup poppy seeds
2 large eggs, beaten
³/₄ cup whole milk

1. Preheat the oven to 400°F. Grease a large baking sheet and set aside.

2. In a large mixing bowl, whisk together the flour, baking powder, salt, and pepper. Cut the shortening into the flour with a pastry cutter till the mixture is mealy. Add the onion, poppy seeds, eggs, and milk and stir till well blended but sticky.

3. Transfer the dough to a lightly floured work surface and knead till quite smooth, about 2 minutes. Roll out the dough about ¹/₄ inch thick and cut out rounds with a 1¹/₂-inch biscuit cutter. Roll the scraps together and cut out more rounds.

4. Arrange the rounds on the prepared baking sheet about ¹/₂ inch apart and bake in the center of the oven till golden, about 15 minutes. Serve at room temperature.

Hootie's Mystery Biscuits

"Guess why these biscuits are so high and fluffy," my sister challenged at a family beach dinner while the rest of us were trying to figure out the strange but beguiling flavor. When we finally gave up, Hootie informed us that she'd used 7-Up to moisten the dough and in-sisted that the soda helped the biscuits to rise. Not just 7-Up, mind you, but *cold* 7-Up, which had to be added all at once to the dry ingredients and stirred quickly to maintain its gaseous fizzle. Hootie says also that only *cold* Crisco shortening gives these biscuits the right texture, that the dough should be allowed to rest a few minutes after being rolled out, and that the biscuits must be thick. Obviously, my sister is very serious about biscuit making.

Makes about 1 dozen biscuits

2 cups all-purpose flour
4 teaspoons baking powder
1 teaspoon salt
$1/4$ cup chilled vegetable shortening
$3/4$ cup chilled 7-Up soda
$1/4$ cup ($1/2$ stick) butter or margarine, melted

1. Preheat the oven to 450°F.

2. In a large mixing bowl, whisk together the flour, baking powder, and salt. Add the shortening and cut it in with a pastry cutter till the mixture is mealy. Add the 7-Up all at once and stir with a fork just till the dry ingredients are evenly moistened.

3. Transfer the dough to a lightly floured work surface and knead about 8 times. Roll out the dough $3/4$ inch thick and let rest for 5 minutes. Cut out rounds with a 2-inch biscuit cutter. Roll the scraps together and cut out more rounds.

4. Arrange the rounds on a baking sheet about $1/2$ inch apart. Brush the rounds with the melted butter and bake in the upper third of the oven till golden brown, 10 to 12 minutes. Serve immediately.

Glazed Mustard Biscuits

Talk about something that's truly great with baked hams and pork roasts—or, for that matter, any dish featuring ham or pork. When I bake a majestic country ham for a festive dinner, these biscuits are an automatic accompaniment, and what I love to do later is break open the biscuits, stuff the halves with ham morsels, and serve them for brunch with various egg dishes. In any case, the biscuits are always best when served as hot as possible. Please don't make these biscuits with that ghastly ballpark mustard— only Dijon style.

Makes about 16 biscuits

$3/4$ **cup half-and-half**
2 tablespoons Dijon mustard
2 cups all-purpose flour
2 teaspoons baking powder
1 teaspoon salt
$1/4$ **cup chilled vegetable shortening**

1. Preheat the oven to 425°F.

2. In a small mixing bowl, combine the half-and-half and mustard, whisk briskly till well blended, and set aside.

3. In a large mixing bowl, whisk together the flour, baking powder, and salt. Add the shortening and cut it in with a pastry cutter or rub with your fingertips till the mixture is mealy. Add about $1/2$ cup of the cream-mustard mixture and stir till the dough is just blended but still slightly sticky.

4. Transfer the dough to a lightly floured work surface and knead about 8 times. Pat out $1/2$ inch thick and cut out rounds with a 2-inch biscuit cutter. Pat the scraps together and cut out more rounds.

5. Arrange the rounds on a baking sheet about 1 inch apart. Brush the tops with the remaining cream-mustard glaze and bake in the upper third of the oven till golden, 12 to 15 minutes.

Honeyed Cornmeal-Chive Biscuits

David Waltuck, owner of New York's celebrated Chanterelle restaurant, is one of the most inspired chefs in America, and while most of the breads served to customers can be pretty sophisticated, the cornmeal-onion biscuits he often makes for staff meals couldn't be more simple and yet unusual. The touch of honey is brilliant, but since his biscuits are a little too dry for my taste, I've added a little heavy cream. Also, for a slightly more delicate texture, I use chives instead of onions and prefer white cornmeal to yellow.

Makes 1 dozen large biscuits

2 cups white cornmeal

1 cup all-purpose flour

3 tablespoons baking powder

1 1/2 teaspoons salt

3 tablespoons chilled butter, cut into bits

1/4 cup minced fresh chives

1 cup half-and-half

1/2 cup heavy cream

2 tablespoons butter, melted and cooled

2 tablespoons honey

1. Preheat the oven to 400°F. Lightly grease a baking sheet and set aside.

2. In a large mixing bowl, whisk together the cornmeal, flour, baking powder, and salt. Add the butter and rub it in with your fingertips till the mixture is just crumbly. Add the chives and stir till well blended.

3. In a small mixing bowl, whisk together the half-and-half, cream, melted butter, and honey till well blended. Add to the dry mixture and stir till just moistened.

4. Transfer the dough to a lightly floured work surface and knead about 8 times. Divide the dough into 12 equal pieces and pat each piece into a flat, round biscuit.

5. Arrange the biscuits on the prepared baking sheet about 1/2 inch apart and bake in the upper third of the oven till lightly browned, about 20 minutes. Serve hot or at room temperature.

Whole Wheat Bacon Biscuits

These are the biscuits that Craig Claiborne once served for breakfast at his home in East Hampton on Long Island, informing guests that he found them to be almost as good as his Mississippi mother's biscuit muffins. The biscuits are a bit heavy, but the flavor imparted by the bacon and bacon grease is inimitable. Watch the biscuits carefully after about 15 minutes of baking to make sure they don't overbrown.

Makes about 16 biscuits

3 strips lean bacon
1 cup whole wheat flour
1 cup all-purpose flour
1 tablespoon baking powder
$1/2$ teaspoon salt
$1/4$ cup chilled vegetable shortening
1 cup whole milk

1. Preheat the oven to 425°F.

2. In a medium-size skillet, fry the bacon over moderate heat till crisp, drain on paper towels, and reserve 1 tablespoon of the grease. Crumble the bacon and set aside.

3. In a large mixing bowl, whisk together both flours, the baking powder, and salt. Add the shortening and cut it in with a pastry cutter till the mixture is mealy. Add the crumbled bacon and reserved tablespoon bacon grease and stir till well blended. Add the milk and stir just till the dough is soft.

4. Transfer the dough to a lightly floured work surface and knead 4 to 5 times. Pat out $1/2$ inch thick and cut out rounds with a 2-inch biscuit cutter. Pat the scraps together and cut out more rounds.

5. Arrange the rounds on a baking sheet about 1 inch apart and bake in the upper third of the oven till golden brown, about 15 minutes.

Maine Clam Biscuits

These distinctive biscuit "sandwiches" come from a Rockland, Maine, community cookbook and illustrate Yankee ingenuity like few other breads I know. Generally, the biscuits are leavened with cream of tartar instead of baking powder, very little shortening is used, and they are served traditionally at Sunday lunch with . . . ketchup! Do try to find the freshest, smallest, tenderest clams possible for these biscuits.

Makes about 8 biscuits

2 cups all-purpose flour
2¹/₂ teaspoons cream of tartar
1 teaspoon baking soda
¹/₂ teaspoon salt
1 teaspoon sugar
2 tablespoons chilled vegetable shortening
1 cup whole milk
1 pint fresh clams, drained and finely chopped
Salt and black pepper to taste
3 tablespoons butter, cut into bits

1. Preheat the oven to 425°F. Lightly grease a baking sheet and set aside.

2. In a large mixing bowl, whisk together the flour, cream of tartar, baking soda, salt, and sugar. Add the shortening and rub it in with your fingertips till mealy. Gradually add the milk, stirring the mixture just till a soft, sticky dough forms.

3. Transfer the dough to a lightly floured work surface and knead 4 to 5 times. Roll out about ¹/₂ inch thick and cut out rounds with a 2-inch biscuit cutter. Roll the scraps together and cut out more rounds.

4. Arrange the rounds on the prepared baking sheet. Spoon equal amounts of the clams on half the rounds, season each with salt and pepper, and top each with a bit of butter. Moisten the edges of the rounds with water, top the clams with the remaining rounds, press the edges to seal, and bake in the upper third of the oven till golden brown, 15 to 20 minutes.

Spiced Pumpkin Biscuits

Like most pumpkin dishes, which are pretty bland without the help of assertive flavorings, these biscuits depend a good deal on brown sugar and spices for character. (You might also add about $1/8$ teaspoon pure vanilla extract to the pumpkin-yogurt mixture.) Since pumpkin also tends to make the biscuits rather heavy, I much prefer margarine to butter in this recipe since it's considerably lighter. Even with all the doctoring, the biscuits have that distinctive pumpkin flavor and color, and they're particularly appropriate for Thanksgiving dinner.

Makes 16 to 18 biscuits

2 cups all-purpose flour
4 teaspoons baking powder
$1/2$ teaspoon baking soda
$1/2$ teaspoon salt
2 tablespoons firmly packed light brown sugar
$1/2$ teaspoon ground nutmeg
$1/2$ teaspoon ground allspice
$1/4$ cup ($1/2$ stick) chilled margarine, cut into bits
1 cup canned pumpkin puree
$1/4$ cup plain yogurt (don't use lowfat or nonfat)

1. Preheat the oven to 425°F.

2. In a large mixing bowl, whisk together the flour, baking powder, baking soda, salt, brown sugar, nutmeg, and allspice. Add the margarine and rub it in with your fingertips till the mixture is mealy. In a small mixing bowl, stir together the pumpkin puree and yogurt till well blended, add to the dry mixture, and stir till the dough is sticky, adding a little more yogurt if necessary.

3. Transfer the dough to a lightly floured work surface and knead about 8 times. Pat out $1/2$ inch thick and cut out rounds with a 2-inch biscuit cutter. Pat the scraps together and cut out more rounds.

4. Arrange the rounds on a baking sheet about 1 inch apart and bake in the upper third of the oven till golden, about 12 minutes.

Georgia Pecan-Molasses Biscuits

Most Southerners frown on any sweet biscuit, but when a journalist I know in Atlanta served these full-flavored, flaky beauties made with lard and just a little molasses, I couldn't help but notice that every single one was gone at the end of a meal attended exclusively by Confederates. Do try to use unsulfured molasses, which has full cane flavor and a more delicate texture than other varieties.

Makes about 16 biscuits

2 cups all-purpose flour
2 tablespoons firmly packed light brown sugar
1 tablespoon baking powder
$^1/_2$ teaspoon baking soda
$^1/_2$ teaspoon salt
$^1/_4$ cup chilled lard, cut into pieces
$^1/_2$ cup finely chopped pecans
1 cup buttermilk
2 tablespoons unsulfured molasses

1. Preheat the oven to 425°F.

2. In a large mixing bowl, whisk together the flour, brown sugar, baking powder, baking soda, and salt. Add the lard and rub it in with your fingertips till the mixture is mealy. Add the pecans and stir till well blended. In a small mixing bowl, beat together the buttermilk and molasses till well blended, add to the dry mixture, and stir just till the dough is sticky.

3. Transfer the dough to a lightly floured work surface and knead about 8 times. Pat out $^1/_2$ inch thick and cut out rounds with a 2-inch biscuit cutter. Pat the scraps together and cut out more rounds.

4. Arrange the rounds on a baking sheet about 1 inch apart and bake in the upper third of the oven till golden, 12 to 15 minutes.

New Hampshire Vanilla Biscuits

I've never been to the Peter Christian's taverns in Hanover or Keene, New Hampshire, but I judge that the American dishes served in those locations are just as traditional and delicious as the ones found in New London. The tavern prides itself on its freshly baked biscuits, and while the savory ones that accompany various meats with gravy are memorable, the unusual, creamy vanilla ones dripping with butter and topped with fresh fruit and whipped cream are worthy of a special visit. Use every ounce of butter indicated and, for the right texture, cut the butter into the dry ingredients only till the mixture looks like coarse oatmeal. Take care not to overbake these biscuits, which should be just golden and soft inside.

Makes about 1 dozen biscuits

2 1/2 **cups all-purpose flour**
1 1/2 **tablespoons baking powder**
1/2 **teaspoon salt**
1 **tablespoon sugar**
1 **cup (2 sticks) chilled butter, cut into pieces**
1 **cup half-and-half**
1/2 **teaspoon pure vanilla extract**

1. Preheat the oven to 425°F. Lightly flour a large baking sheet.

2. In a large mixing bowl, whisk together the flour, baking powder, salt, and sugar. Add the butter and cut it in with a pastry cutter till the mixture resembles oatmeal. Add the half-and-half and vanilla and stir just till the dry ingredients are moistened.

3. Transfer the dough to a lightly floured work surface and knead briefly to form a large ball. Flatten the ball with the palm of your hand, then roll out quickly 3/4 inch thick and cut out rounds with a 2 1/2-inch biscuit cutter. Roll the scraps together and cut out more rounds.

4. Arrange the rounds on the prepared baking sheet about 1/2 inch apart and bake in the center of the oven till golden, 12 to 15 minutes.

Maple Pinwheel Biscuits

Pinwheel biscuits are popular breakfast items in both New England and the Upper Midwest, a regional variation on coffee cakes that takes on a whole new identity when biscuit dough is used. I've also had these biscuits made with brown sugar and ground cinnamon, but, frankly, I think such added flavorings detract from the luscious maple syrup. Some cooks also add a little jam to the filling, but again, I find that too to be slight overkill. Maybe you'll care to experiment and decide. Notice that the dough is never kneaded for these biscuits and that they are baked just till they're cooked through and still soft and sticky.

Makes about 8 large biscuits

2 cups all-purpose flour

2 teaspoons baking powder

1/2 teaspoon salt

2 tablespoons sugar

6 tablespoons (3/4 stick) chilled butter, cut into bits

2/3 cup whole milk

1/2 cup chopped walnuts

1 cup pure maple syrup

1. Preheat the oven to 425°F. Grease a 7 x 5 x 3-inch baking pan and set aside.

2. In a large mixing bowl, whisk together the flour, baking powder, salt, and sugar. Add half the butter bits and cut in with a pastry cutter till the mixture is mealy. Gradually add the milk and stir till a soft dough forms.

3. Transfer the dough to a lightly floured work surface and roll out into a rectangle 1/2 inch thick. Dot the dough with the remaining butter and sprinkle 1/4 cup of the nuts evenly over the top. Roll tightly lengthwise as for a jelly roll and cut the roll into 1-inch-thick slices.

4. Arrange the slices in the prepared pan, drizzle the maple syrup evenly over the tops, sprinkle the remaining 1/4 cup nuts over the tops, and bake in the center of the oven till cooked through and sticky, 15 to 20 minutes.

Yankee Maple Syrup Biscuits

Nothing could be more indicative of robust, no-nonsense Yankee baking than these sweet, slightly chewy, hand-formed biscuits that are relished at breakfast and with tea throughout northern New England and the Upper Midwest. So devoted are the folks around Green Bay, Wisconsin, to baking breads with maple syrup, in fact, that every May they hold a special festival that features all sorts of biscuits, muffins, pancakes, and dumplings prepared with maple syrup. Some Vermont cooks actually form thicker biscuits and bake them a bit longer till they're almost cake-like, and others might add ¼ teaspoon ground ginger or nutmeg to the dough, as well as press raisins or chopped nuts into the tops before baking. By no means leave out the bacon grease, which not only balances the sweetness but gives the biscuits a very subtle flavor.

Makes about 1 dozen biscuits

½ cup pure maple syrup
¼ cup sugar
¼ cup vegetable shortening, melted and cooled
1 tablespoon bacon grease
2½ cups all-purpose flour
½ heaping teaspoon baking soda
½ teaspoon salt
½ cup buttermilk

1. Preheat the oven to 400°F. Grease a baking sheet and set aside.

2. In a small mixing bowl, beat the maple syrup, sugar, melted shortening, and bacon grease together till well blended.

3. In a large mixing bowl, whisk together 2 cups of the flour, the baking soda, and salt, add the buttermilk, and stir till the dry ingredients are just moistened. Add the maple syrup mixture and stir till a soft dough forms, adding more of the flour if necessary.

4. Transfer to a lightly floured work surface and knead about 8 times. With well-floured hands, form the dough into biscuits about 2½ inches in diameter and ½ inch thick, arrange them on the prepared baking sheet about 1 inch apart, and bake in the center of the oven till golden brown, 15 to 20 minutes.

Kansas Fruit Biscuits

Years ago, I came across this enticing biscuit recipe in the *Household Searchlight Recipe Book*, published back in 1941 by an organization in Topeka, Kansas, devoted to "helping every woman who finds herself responsible for the management of a home and the care of children." I find the folding and stuffing technique fascinating, and the biscuits are, without doubt, some of the most delicious I've ever put in my mouth. What the dear ladies did with the leftover scraps of stuffed dough, of course, is anybody's guess. Notice that the biscuits are not baked very long and should be slightly moist inside.

Makes about 10 biscuits

2 cups all-purpose flour
4 teaspoons baking powder
$1/2$ teaspoon salt
3 tablespoons chilled vegetable shortening
$3/4$ cup whole milk
2 tablespoons butter, melted
2 tablespoons firmly packed light brown sugar
$1/2$ teaspoon ground cinnamon
$1/2$ cup finely chopped dark raisins

1. Preheat the oven to 425°F. Grease a baking sheet and set aside.

2. In a large mixing bowl, whisk together the flour, baking powder, and salt. Add the shortening and cut it in with a pastry cutter till the mixture is mealy. Add the milk and stir with a fork till a soft ball of dough forms.

3. Transfer the dough to a lightly floured work surface and knead about 8 times. Pat out the dough $1/2$ inch thick, brush half the dough with the melted butter, and top the buttered half with the brown sugar, cinnamon, and finally, the raisins. Fold the other half over the top, press down slightly, pinch the edges together, and cut out rounds with a $2^{1}/2$-inch biscuit cutter.

4. Arrange the rounds on the prepared baking sheet about 1 inch apart, and bake in the center of the oven till golden, about 12 minutes. Serve hot or at room temperature.

Drop Biscuits

Drop biscuits, which are often called batter biscuits in the Upper Midwest, differ from standard raised biscuits in a number of ways. First, they are usually leavened with both baking powder and eggs but have a less tender structure since they generally contain less fat. The dough must be quite wet and, to maintain the right loose texture, the dough is never kneaded or rolled. If the dough appears too dense after stirring, simply add a little more liquid—or possibly another beaten egg—till the consistency is almost like a batter.

Always grease baking sheets for drop biscuits and drop them at least 1 inch apart—more, if the dough is particularly wet. Don't expect these biscuits to be even like patted or rolled out and cut biscuits, not unless you drop them in a muffin tin. Generally, the tops should be crispy to crunchy.

Drop biscuits can be either savory or sweet, though traditionally the vast majority are fairly sweet. Essentially, the dough for any savory biscuit can be transformed into one that can be dropped by reducing the fat and adding more liquid, and remember that some savory drop biscuit doughs (Chive Drop Biscuits, on page 62, for example) make nice crusts for pot pies. Likewise, certain sweetened drop biscuit doughs, such as that for Spiced Honey Drop Biscuits, on page 68, might well be used to top fruit pies and cobblers.

Best of all, drop biscuits are both easy and fun to make— and a great way to get young children interested in biscuit making.

Chive Drop Biscuits

This is the basic formula for savory drop biscuits, though in some areas of the country the shortening might be left out altogether since there is considerable fat in the cream and egg yolk. Chives are my favorite flavoring for this biscuit, but you can substitute 2 tablespoons of any minced onion, parsley, fresh herbs, prepared horseradish, or grated cheese. This dough can also be used to make a crust for meat and poultry pot pies.

Makes 18 to 20 biscuits

2 cups all-purpose flour
2¹/₂ teaspoons baking powder
1 teaspoon salt
2 tablespoons chilled vegetable shortening
1 cup heavy cream
1 large egg, beaten
2 tablespoons minced fresh chives

1. Preheat the oven to 425°F. Grease a large baking sheet and set aside.

2. In a large mixing bowl, whisk together the flour, baking powder, and salt. Add the shortening and rub with your fingers till the mixture is mealy. In a medium-size mixing bowl, whisk or beat the cream with an electric mixer till almost stiff peaks form and fold into the dry mixture. Add the egg and chives and stir till the dough is blended but still slightly wet, adding a little extra cream or another beaten egg if necessary.

3. Drop the dough by rounded tablespoons onto the prepared baking sheet at least 1 inch apart and bake in the upper third of the oven till golden brown, 13 to 15 minutes. Serve hot.

Sour Cream and Dill Drop Biscuits

These simple "drops" are ideal to serve with virtually any seafood—broiled or grilled fish, baked shrimp or crabmeat dishes, chilled seafood salads, and certainly fried shrimp, clams, or calamari. Do feel free to reduce the amount of dill if your passion for the herb is not as intense as mine, and do watch these biscuits carefully to make sure they remain slightly creamy.

Makes 18 to 20 biscuits

2 cups all-purpose flour

1 tablespoon baking powder

1 teaspoon salt

1 teaspoon sugar

$^1/_2$ teaspoon baking soda

2 tablespoons chilled butter, cut into bits

$^1/_4$ cup snipped fresh dill

$^1/_2$ cup sour cream (don't use lowfat or nonfat)

$^1/_2$ cup whole milk

1 large egg, beaten

1. Preheat the oven to 425°F. Grease a large baking sheet and set aside.

2. In a large mixing bowl, whisk together the flour, baking powder, salt, sugar, and baking soda. Add the butter and rub it into the flour with your fingertips till the mixture is mealy. Add the dill, sour cream, milk, and egg and stir just till a wet, sticky dough forms.

3. Drop the dough by rounded tablespoons onto the prepared baking sheet about 1 inch apart and bake in the center of the oven till golden, 12 to 15 minutes.

Rosemary-Garlic Drop Biscuits

I suppose you could use about a teaspoon of dried rosemary and half a teaspoon of garlic powder for these "drops," but if you want a biscuit really bursting with flavor, do try to use the fresh ingredients—especially when the summer herb garden is flourishing. Any other fresh herb, of course, could be substituted for the rosemary, as could a proportionate combination of herbs. I like to serve this type of biscuit with both hearty meat stews and grilled steaks. If you don't have self-rising flour, simply whisk 4 teaspoons baking powder and 1 teaspoon salt into 2 cups bleached all-purpose flour.

Makes about 1½ dozen biscuits

2 cups self-rising flour
1 tablespoon minced fresh rosemary leaves
1 teaspoon minced garlic
½ teaspoon black pepper
1 cup whole milk
¼ cup olive oil

1. Preheat the oven to 425°F. Grease a baking sheet and set aside.

2. In a large mixing bowl, mix together thoroughly the flour, rosemary, garlic, and pepper. Add the milk and olive oil and stir just till a very soft and still slightly wet dough forms.

3. Drop the dough by rounded tablespoons onto the prepared baking sheet about 1½ inches apart and bake in the upper third of the oven till golden brown, 12 to 15 minutes. Serve hot or at room temperature.

biscuit bonus

Always check the date on self-rising flour to make sure it hasn't expired. Biscuits made with outdated self-rising flour will not rise properly.

Parmesan-Herb Drop Biscuits

You can certainly prepare these herby cheese biscuits like most other drop biscuits and serve them at brunches or virtually any meal, but a clever idea is to mix the dry ingredients, tie them securely in a cellophane bag, and give the bag as a gift with directions on a colorful card on how to add the liquid ingredients, mix the dough, and drop the biscuits. No gift is more unusual, and it's a nice way to encourage friends (and youngsters) to begin making drop biscuits. The recipe is simplicity itself.

Makes about 1 1/2 dozen biscuits

2 cups self-rising flour
1/2 cup finely grated genuine Parmesan cheese
1/2 teaspoon dried basil, crumbled
1/4 teaspoon dried thyme, crumbled
1 cup whole milk
1 large egg, beaten
2 tablespoons butter, melted and cooled

1. Preheat the oven to 425°F. Grease a baking sheet and set aside.

2. In a large mixing bowl, mix thoroughly the flour, cheese, basil, and thyme. Add the milk, egg, and butter and stir just till a soft but still slightly wet dough forms.

3. Drop the dough by rounded tablespoons onto the prepared baking sheet about 1 inch apart and bake in the upper third of the oven till golden brown, 12 to 15 minutes. Serve warm or at room temperature.

> "[We ate] a dish of biscuits pounded fine, salt beef cut into small pieces, and a few potatoes, all boiled up together and seasoned with pepper."
>
> —RICHARD HENRY DANA,
> *Two Years Before the Mast*,
> 1840

Chile-Cheese Drop Biscuits

Other than ordinary corn or wheat tortillas, I was always at a loss as to what bread to serve with Mexican or Tex-Mex food till a rather grand lady I know in Houston had her Mexican cook bake a batch of these tangy drop biscuits. You can use a couple of finely diced fresh jalapeños instead of the canned chiles, and do feel free to adjust the amount of garlic according to your taste.

Makes at least 16 biscuits

2 cups self-rising flour
1 teaspoon baking soda
2 tablespoons chilled vegetable shortening
1 cup shredded Monterey Jack cheese
One 4-ounce can diced green chiles, well drained
1 garlic clove, minced
³/4 cup buttermilk
1 large egg, beaten
2 tablespoons margarine, melted

1. Preheat the oven to 425°F. Grease a large baking sheet and set aside.

2. In a large mixing bowl, whisk together the flour and baking soda. Add the shortening and cut it into the flour with a pastry cutter till the mixture is crumbly. Add the cheese, chiles, and garlic and stir till well blended. Add the buttermilk and egg and stir till the dough is well blended but still slightly wet.

3. Drop the dough by rounded tablespoons onto the prepared baking sheet about 1 inch apart and bake in the upper third of the oven till golden brown, 12 to 15 minutes. Brush the biscuits with the melted margarine and serve warm.

Parmesan-Chutney Drop Biscuits

I find the tangy-sweet contrast in these biscuits utterly captivating, as well as the way the cream and egg smooth out the cheese and chutney. The biscuits are an unusual surprise served at casual brunches featuring any egg dishes, and I like to drop them into a baking dish, which can go directly from the oven to the buffet or dining table.

Makes about 1½ dozen biscuits

2 cups all-purpose flour
2 teaspoons baking powder
½ teaspoon salt
2 tablespoons chilled butter, cut into bits
1 cup freshly grated genuine Parmesan cheese
3 tablespoons Major Grey's chutney, finely chopped
½ cup whole milk
2 tablespoons heavy cream
1 large egg, beaten

1. Preheat the oven to 425°F. Grease a large baking dish and set aside.

2. In a large mixing bowl, whisk together the flour, baking powder, and salt. Add the butter and rub it into the flour with your fingertips till the mixture feels mealy. Add the cheese and chutney and stir till well blended. Add the milk, cream, and egg and stir just till a wet, sticky dough forms.

3. Drop the dough by rounded tablespoons into the prepared baking dish about 1 inch apart and bake till golden brown, about 15 minutes.

Spiced Honey Drop Biscuits

Few breads, in my opinion, go better with any baked ham or ham preparation than these spicy, slightly buttery drop biscuits enhanced with a little honey that a lady outside Chicago once served at a memorable lakeside luncheon. I must say that sometimes I like to add one or two teaspoons of Dijon mustard to the buttermilk mixture for a bit of tang, in which case I might delete the honey. This is truly one drop biscuit you'll have fun experimenting with.

Makes about 16 biscuits

2 cups all-purpose flour
1 tablespoon baking powder
1 teaspoon baking soda
1 teaspoon ground cinnamon
1 teaspoon ground allspice
$1/2$ teaspoon salt
3 tablespoons chilled butter, cut into bits
$1/4$ cup buttermilk
$1/4$ cup water
2 tablespoons honey
1 large egg

1. Preheat the oven to 425°F. Grease a large baking sheet and set aside.

2. In a large mixing bowl, whisk together the flour, baking powder, baking soda, cinnamon, allspice, and salt. Add the butter and rub it into the flour with your fingertips till the mixture is mealy. In a small mixing bowl, whisk together the buttermilk, water, honey, and egg till well blended, add to the dry mixture, and stir just till a wet dough forms, adding a little more water if necessary.

3. Drop the dough by heaping tablespoons onto the prepared baking sheet about $1^1/2$ inches apart and bake in the upper third of the oven till golden, 12 to 15 minutes.

Spiced Cream Drop Biscuits

Because of all the heavy cream, these large drop biscuits need no additional fat to give them supple texture, but they should be baked slowly to maintain their creaminess. Serve these biscuits for breakfast slathered with butter and jam, and you'll never again even think of bagels or heavy pastries. If you prefer a more even shape, the biscuits can also be baked in a muffin tin

Makes about 1 dozen biscuits

2$1/2$ **cups all-purpose flour**
1 **tablespoon baking powder**
1 **tablespoon sugar**
1 **teaspoon salt**
$1/2$ **teaspoon ground mace or nutmeg**
2 **cups heavy cream**
$1/2$ **teaspoon pure vanilla extract**

1. Preheat the oven to 350°F. Grease a large baking sheet and set aside.

2. In a large mixing bowl, whisk together the flour, baking powder, sugar, salt, and mace. Add the cream and vanilla and stir just till a soft but still wet dough forms.

3. Drop shallow $1/4$ cups of batter onto the prepared baking sheet about 1$1/2$ inches apart and bake in the center of the oven till the tops are pale golden and the bottoms golden brown, 18 to 20 minutes. Serve hot.

biscuit bonus

There's no need to bother sifting dry ingredients for biscuits. Simply stir them quickly and steadily with a wire whisk.

Cinnamon-Pecan Drop Biscuits

Made partly with cake flour, these are true batter biscuits that will remind you of tiny breakfast coffee cakes. The dough for these "drops" should be just wet enough to cling to the sides of the bowl when stirred. These also make nice tea biscuits.

Makes about 2½ dozen biscuits

1 cup all-purpose flour

1 cup cake flour

2 teaspoons baking powder

½ teaspoon salt

¼ cup sugar

3 tablespoons chilled butter, cut into bits

1 cup whole milk

1 large egg, beaten

½ cup finely chopped pecans

⅛ teaspoon ground cinnamon

1. Preheat the oven to 425°F. Grease 2 baking sheets and set aside.

2. In a large mixing bowl, whisk together the two flours, baking powder, salt, and 3 tablespoons of the sugar. Add the butter and cut it into the flour with a pastry cutter till the mixture is mealy. Add the milk and egg and stir till the flour is dampened. Add the pecans and stir till the dough is softly wet and clings to the sides of the bowl.

3. Drop the dough by rounded teaspoons onto the prepared baking sheets about 1 inch apart. In a small bowl, mix together the remaining 1 tablespoon sugar and the cinnamon, sprinkle the mixture evenly over the mounds of dough, and bake in the upper third of the oven till golden, 12 to 13 minutes.

In much of the South, the word "biscuit" is still often used only in the singular when referring to more than one biscuit, e.g., "Those are the best biscuit I've ever put in my mouth."

Coconut-Vanilla Drop Biscuits

While these rather dainty biscuits are perfect for wedding receptions, afternoon socials, and ice cream parties, they're actually so good that I like to serve them just by themselves with coffee after an elaborate dinner. When toasting the coconut, do watch it carefully to make sure it doesn't burn in the least.

Makes about 20 biscuits

$3/4$ cup frozen unsweetened flaked coconut (available in health food stores and some supermarkets)

2 cups all-purpose flour

2 tablespoons sugar

2 teaspoons baking powder

$1/2$ teaspoon salt

2 tablespoons chilled vegetable shortening

1 cup whole milk

1 large egg, beaten

$1/2$ teaspoon pure vanilla extract

1. Preheat the oven to 300°F. Spread the still-frozen coconut on a large baking sheet and toast in the oven, stirring often, till golden, about 30 minutes. Remove to a bowl and let cool.

2. Increase the oven temperature to 425°F. Grease the baking sheet and set aside.

3. In a large mixing bowl, whisk together the coconut, flour, sugar, baking powder, and salt. Add the shortening and cut it into the flour with a pastry cutter till the mixture is crumbly. In a small mixing bowl, whisk together the milk, egg, and vanilla, add to the dry ingredients, and stir just till the dough is very soft and still slightly wet.

4. Drop the dough by scant tablespoons onto the prepared baking sheet about 1 inch apart and bake in the upper third of the oven till golden, about 12 minutes. Serve hot or at room temperature.

Oatmeal-Raisin Drop Biscuits

I'll hold up these buttery biscuits any day to ordinary oatmeal-raisin cookies and, frankly, they're lots more fun to make. Using this basic formula, you can substitute for the raisins everything from crushed almonds to minced dates or dried apricots to finely chopped apples. This dough also makes delicious chocolate chip biscuits (minus the cinnamon), though they can be a bit messy.

Makes 18 to 20 biscuits

1 1/2 cups all-purpose flour
2 tablespoons sugar
1 tablespoon baking powder
1 teaspoon salt
1 teaspoon ground cinnamon
1/2 cup (1 stick) chilled butter, cut into bits
1/2 cup quick-cooking oats
1/2 cup seedless golden raisins
1 cup whole milk
1 large egg, beaten

1. Preheat the oven to 425°F. Grease a large baking sheet and set aside.

2. In a large mixing bowl, whisk together the flour, sugar, baking powder, salt, and cinnamon. Add the butter and rub it into the flour with your fingertips till the mixture is mealy. Stir in the oats and raisins till well blended, add the milk and egg, and stir just till a wet, sticky dough forms.

3. Drop the dough by rounded tablespoons onto the prepared baking sheet about 1 inch apart and bake in the center of the oven till golden, 12 to 15 minutes.

Old Dominion Ginger Drop Biscuits

From what friends of mine in Roanoke have told me, these small ginger biscuits (or, as some call them, "Old Dominion drops") must have been a Virginia specialty since the late nineteenth century. They're like ginger snaps in that they're leavened only with an egg and enough baking soda to neutralize the acid in the molasses, and, traditionally, they're dropped only by teaspoons, not table-spoons. Serve the biscuits with ice cream or fresh fruit for dessert, and store the extras in tightly covered containers for up to two weeks.

Makes about 40 biscuits

2 cups all-purpose flour
2 teaspoons baking soda
2 teaspoons ground ginger
$^1/_2$ teaspoon ground cloves
$^1/_2$ teaspoon salt
$^1/_2$ cup (1 stick) butter, softened
1 cup sugar
1 large egg
$^1/_4$ cup unsulfured molasses

1. Preheat the oven to 375°F. Grease 2 baking sheets and set aside.

2. In a large mixing bowl, whisk together the flour, baking soda, ginger, cloves, and salt. In a medium-size mixing bowl, cream the butter and sugar together with an electric mixer or wooden spoon, add the egg and molasses, and beat till well blended. Add to the dry ingredients and stir just till the dough is soft but still slightly wet.

3. Drop the dough by rounded teaspoons onto the prepared baking sheets about 2 inches apart and bake in the upper third of the oven till crispy golden brown, about 20 minutes. Let cool completely before serving.

Cocktail and Tea Biscuits

Of all the treats and delicacies I serve at cocktail parties and afternoon teas, the popularity of none equals that of the savory and sweet biscuits that I usually make in embarrassingly large numbers. Perhaps it's my Southern heritage and our long tradition of plying guests with plenty of tasty food, but the truth is that I (like my mother) can't imagine not keeping tin after tin, or freezer-container after container, of aromatic Parmesan biscuits, sausage-pecan biscuits, delicate orange tea biscuits, and who knows what other styles that come in so handy when people drop by for cocktails or tea.

Most, but not all, of these biscuits can be made in quantity and either stored in airtight containers for a couple of weeks or frozen till ready to pop into the oven. Just use your common sense as to which ones keep well and which are best served shortly after they're baked. Obviously, biscuits involving smoked salmon and fresh caviar, lots of cream, or overly sticky glazes are not intended to sit around for long, but others can be made well in advance and kept till they start to dry out or lose their savor. Admittedly, I also love to have a number of these biscuits around for snacks.

Benne Biscuit Wafers

In and around Charleston, South Carolina, sesame seeds are called benne, which are traditionally utilized—raw or toasted—in everything from soups and salads to cookies and ice creams to crackers and biscuits. Ordinary thin, dry benne wafers, often called "cocktailers," are sold everywhere in every style imaginable, but the only time I ever saw these slightly soft biscuit wafers was at a very stylish luncheon given by one of the town's grande dames who had a brilliant black cook. Look for hulled raw seeds in natural food shops instead of the less fresh and more expensive ones in jars found in some supermarkets. Stored in airtight containers, benne seeds keep for months.

Makes about 40 wafers

$1/4$ **cup benne (sesame) seeds**
1 cup all-purpose flour
1 teaspoon baking powder
$1/4$ **teaspoon baking soda**
$1/4$ **teaspoon salt**
Cayenne pepper to taste
$1/4$ **cup ($1/2$ stick) chilled butter or margarine, cut into bits**
2 tablespoons plain yogurt (don't use lowfat or nonfat)
2 tablespoons whole milk

1. Preheat the oven to 350°F.

2. Scatter the benne seeds evenly on a baking sheet and toast in the oven, stirring, till golden brown, about 10 minutes. Let cool. Increase the oven temperature to 400°F.

3. In a large mixing bowl, whisk together the flour, baking powder, baking soda, salt, and cayenne. Add the butter and rub it into the flour with your fingertips till the mixture is mealy. Add the toasted benne seeds, yogurt, and milk and stir till the dough is smooth.

4. Transfer the dough to a lightly floured work surface, roll out about $1/4$ inch thick, and cut out rounds with a 1-inch biscuit cutter. Roll the scraps together and cut out more rounds.

5. Arrange the rounds on a large baking sheet about $1/2$ inch apart, and bake in the upper third of the oven till golden and slightly crisp, about 10 minutes. Let cool, then store in an airtight container up to about 2 weeks.

Parmesan Biscuits

Since the heavy cream contains sufficient fat, these tangy biscuits require no butter or shortening. The biscuits are equally delicious made with sharp, well-aged cheddar or finely crumbled blue cheese, and when I intend to pass them at cocktail parties, I make them smaller—usually with a 1¹/₂-inch cutter. Ditto if I simply want them around as a snack. This is one time when it's obligatory to use only freshly grated genuine Parmesan cheese. The biscuits keep well in an airtight container for up to two weeks.

Makes about 1 dozen biscuits

2 cups all-purpose flour
1 tablespoon baking powder
¹/₂ teaspoon salt
1¹/₂ cups freshly grated genuine Parmesan cheese
1¹/₄ cups heavy cream

1. Preheat the oven to 425°F.

2. In a large mixing bowl, whisk together the flour, baking powder, and salt. Add the cheese and stir till well blended. Add the cream and stir the mixture just till it forms a loose dough.

3. Transfer the dough to a lightly floured work surface and knead about 8 times. Pat out the dough ¹/₂ inch thick and cut out rounds with a 2¹/₂-inch biscuit cutter. Pat the scraps together and cut out more rounds.

4. Arrange the rounds on a baking sheet about ¹/₂ inch apart and bake in the upper third of the oven till golden, 13 to 15 minutes.

biscuit bonus

The drier and harder a biscuit is, the longer it will keep without going stale or molding. Soft, fluffy biscuits intended for toasting keep well in the refrigerator up to about five days.

Blue Cheese and Walnut Cocktail Biscuits

My original inspiration for these tangy quick-and-easy cocktail biscuits was a more complicated and time-consuming recipe spotted in a soup cookbook where the dough was chilled overnight before being sliced thinly to produce biscuit crisps. The problem was the crisps were actually too heavy and dry despite all the effort, so I went about modifying the recipe by using self-rising flour, leavening the cheese and walnuts with lard and a little cream of tartar, and simply pressing out bite-size discs with my fingers. The result are biscuits that are flaky, remarkably light, and a cinch to make.

Makes about 20 biscuits

$1^{1}/_{2}$ cups self-rising flour
$^{1}/_{3}$ teaspoon cream of tartar
$^{1}/_{2}$ cup crumbled blue cheese
$^{1}/_{2}$ cup roughly chopped walnuts
3 tablespoons chilled lard, cut into pieces
$^{3}/_{4}$ cup whole milk, or more as needed

1. Preheat the oven to 400°F. Grease a large baking sheet and set aside.

2. In a food processor, combine the flour and cream of tartar and pulse quickly to blend well. Add the cheese, walnuts, and lard and pulse till the mixture is crumbly. Add the milk and pulse just till the dough is loose and still sticky, adding more milk, if necessary.

3. Transfer the dough to a lightly floured work surface and knead 3 to 4 times. With floured hands, roll pieces of dough into balls about the size of large marbles and arrange on the prepared baking sheet about $^{1}/_{2}$ inch apart. Press the balls down slightly with your fingers and bake in the upper third of the oven till golden, about 15 minutes.

Bacon-Cheddar Cocktail Biscuits

The only time I remember ever running out of all-purpose flour was one evening when I was determined to serve these wonderful biscuits at a cocktail party and discovered with alarm that the only flour in the kitchen was a sack of unopened Southern self-rising somebody had brought me. Suffice it to say that the biscuits turned out beautifully, and while I've never gotten into the regular habit of using self-rising flour for biscuits, the experience was rewarding enough to make me think twice. Just never forget that self-rising flour (which is ordinary all-purpose with both baking powder and salt added) must be strictly fresh to be effective. Consider doubling this recipe since the biscuits keep well in an airtight container up to about two weeks and are so handy when friends drop by for a drink.

Makes about 1½ dozen biscuits

½ **pound sliced lean bacon**
2 **cups self-rising flour**
½ **teaspoon baking soda**
Black pepper to taste
⅓ **cup chilled vegetable shortening**
1 **cup grated extra-sharp cheddar cheese**
1 **cup buttermilk**

1. In a large skillet, fry the bacon over moderate heat till crisp, drain on paper towels, crumble finely, and set aside.

2. Preheat the oven to 425°F. Lightly grease a large baking sheet and set aside.

3. In a large mixing bowl, whisk together the flour, baking soda, and pepper. Add the shortening and cut it into the flour with a pastry cutter till the mixture is mealy. Add the bacon, cheese, and buttermilk and stir just till the dry ingredients are well moistened.

4. Transfer the dough to a lightly floured work surface and knead 4 to 5 times. Pat out the dough about ½ inch thick and cut out rounds with a 2-inch biscuit cutter. Pat the scraps together and cut out more rounds.

5. Arrange the rounds on the prepared baking sheet about ½ inch apart and bake in the upper third of the oven till golden, 12 to 15 minutes. Let cool and store in an airtight container for up to 2 weeks.

Pimento-Cheese Cocktail Biscuits

I am never, ever without at least one tin of these luscious, nippy, small biscuits, which make a great snack and are ideal for any cocktail party. The pimentos do add an interesting savor, but if you don't have a jar on hand, the biscuits are almost as delicious without them. For the right crunchy-soft texture, the biscuits need to be baked fairly slowly and never overbrowned. I love my biscuits to have a good kick, but feel free to adjust the cayenne to your (and your guests') taste. Do make sure that your pecans are not rancid. Storing them in the freezer will keep them fresh.

Makes 50 to 55 biscuits

$^1/_2$ pound extra-sharp cheddar cheese
1 cup (2 sticks) butter or margarine, softened and cut into pieces
One 4-ounce jar pimentos, well drained and finely diced
$^1/_4$ teaspoon salt
Big dash of cayenne pepper
2 cups all-purpose flour
50 to 55 pecan halves for topping

1. Preheat the oven to 350°F. Grease 2 baking sheets and set aside.

2. Grate the cheese very finely into a large mixing bowl, add the butter, pimentos, salt, and cayenne, and mix with your hands till well blended. Gradually add the flour and mix with your hands till the dough is firm and smooth, adding a little more flour if necessary.

3. Roll pieces of dough between the palms of your hands into balls the size of large marbles and arrange on the prepared baking sheets about 1 inch apart. Press a pecan half into the center of each and bake in the center of the oven till slightly browned but still fairly soft, about 20 minutes.

4. Let cool completely, then store in an airtight container up to 2 weeks.

Sausage-Pecan Cocktail Biscuits

In many respects, these are the ultimate cocktail biscuits, and if my experience is any indication of their popularity with guests, you won't have a single biscuit left over. Best of all, the unbaked balls of dough can be made in quantity, frozen between layers of waxed paper in airtight containers for up to about a month, then thawed quickly and finished off with the pecans when company is expected. As always, make sure the pecans are not in the least rancid.

Makes about 3 dozen biscuits

$1/2$ **pound bulk pork sausage**

$1/2$ **cup (1 stick) margarine, softened**

1 cup grated extra-sharp cheddar cheese, at room temperature

$3/4$ **cup all-purpose flour**

$1/2$ **teaspoon salt**

36 pecan halves for topping

1. In a large, heavy skillet, break up the sausage and fry over moderate heat till cooked through. Drain on paper towels and, when cool enough to handle, crumble well.

2. In a large mixing bowl, cream the margarine and cheese together with an electric mixer. Add the flour and salt and stir till well blended. Add the sausage, stir till well blended and smooth, cover with plastic wrap, and chill the dough about 30 minutes.

3. Preheat the oven to 375°F.

4. Pinch off small pieces of dough, roll them between your palms into 1-inch balls, flatten each ball slightly with your fingers, and arrange on two baking sheets about 1 inch apart. Press a pecan half into the center of each and bake in the center of the oven till golden brown, 15 to 20 minutes. Serve warm.

Sam's
Cloud
Biscuits

page 18

Smoked Salmon and
Dill Biscuits with
Salmon Caviar

page 84

Texas Chili
on Jalapeño
Buttermilk Biscuits

page 116

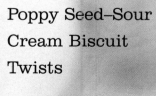

Poppy Seed–Sour
Cream Biscuit
Twists

page 82

Maine
Clam
Biscuits

page 54

Jean's
Sticky
Biscuits

page 130

Spiced
Peach
Shortcake

page 124

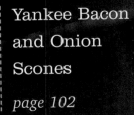

Yankee Bacon
and Onion
Scones

page 102

Cajun Biscuit Sausage Rolls

I guess the reason I've always called these spicy balls "Cajun" is because they were served (with a lethal punch) at a big outdoor crab-and-shrimp boil I once attended in Breaux Bridge, Louisiana. If you've ever been exposed to those sausage balls covered with nothing but a wretched flour-and-water paste, these, made with a leavened biscuit mix, will prove a revelation.

Makes about 2 dozen rolls

1 pound bulk pork sausage
1 teaspoon ground sage
^{1}/2 teaspoon red pepper flakes
Salt and black pepper to taste
Vegetable oil for frying
1^1/2 cups Homemade Biscuit Mix (page 11)
^{1}/2 cup whole milk

1. In a medium-size mixing bowl, combine the sausage, sage, and red pepper flakes, season with salt and black pepper, and stir till the mixture is very smooth. With your hands, form the mixture into small balls about the size of walnuts and place them on a plate.

2. In a deep, heavy saucepan, heat about 1^1/2 inches of oil to 375°F and, in batches, fry the sausage balls till nicely browned on all sides, about 10 minutes. Drain on paper towels and let cool.

3. Preheat the oven to 400°F. Grease a large baking sheet and set aside.

4. In a medium-size mixing bowl, combine the biscuit mix and milk and stir till the dough is smooth. Flour your hands lightly, then wrap each sausage ball in a small piece of dough, smoothing the surface with your fingers. Arrange the balls on the prepared baking sheet about ^{1}/2 inch apart and bake in the center of the oven till golden, about 15 minutes.

Poppy Seed–Sour Cream Biscuit Twists

These biscuit twists are not only fun and easy to make but ever so attractive for both cocktails and tea. Of course, you could sprinkle the tops with anything from sesame seeds to chopped herbs to crushed nuts, but the poppy seeds are a bit different and have a very distinctive flavor. Be sure to flour your hands well when forming the twists.

Makes 16 twists

2 1/2 cups all-purpose flour
1 tablespoon baking powder
1 1/2 teaspoons salt
1/2 teaspoon baking soda
1 cup sour cream (don't use lowfat or nonfat)
2 large eggs, beaten separately
1/4 cup vegetable shortening, melted and cooled
1 tablespoon Dijon mustard
Poppy seeds for sprinkling

1. Preheat the oven to 425°F.

2. In a large mixing bowl, whisk together the flour, baking powder, salt, and baking soda. Add the sour cream, 1 of the eggs, and the shortening and stir till the dough is smooth.

3. Transfer to a lightly floured work surface and knead about 8 times. Roll the dough into a long rope about 2 inches thick and cut it crosswise into 16 pieces. Roll each piece into a rope about 8 inches long, fold each in half, twist each two times, pinching the ends together, and arrange the twists on a large baking sheet about 1 inch apart.

4. In a small bowl, whisk together the remaining egg and the mustard till well blended, brush each twist with the egg wash, sprinkle poppy seeds generously over the tops, and bake in the upper third of the oven till golden and slightly crisp, about 15 minutes.

Taco Biscuit Bites

Since I'd never before owned bottles of dried onion flakes and taco sauce, I balked when I found this recipe developed by the good folks who produce White Lily flour. I nonetheless was curious about the unusual drop biscuits, and suffice it to say that I'm now a bit more tolerant of at least some of those commercial products when they're used only as seasonings in this type of mix. I served the biscuit bites at a pretty snazzy cocktail party, and they were gone in twenty minutes.

Makes about 1 1/2 dozen biscuit bites

2 cups self-rising flour
1/4 cup chilled vegetable shortening
1/4 cup bottled taco sauce
1/2 cup whole milk
1/2 cup shredded extra-sharp cheddar cheese
1 teaspoon onion flakes
1/4 cup (1/2 stick) butter or margarine, melted

1. Preheat the oven to 450°F.

2. In a large mixing bowl, combine the flour and shortening and cut in with a pastry cutter till the shortening is the size of small peas. Add the taco sauce, milk, cheese, and onion flakes and stir till well blended but still slightly wet.

3. Drop the dough by heaping teaspoons onto a large baking sheet or pan about 1 inch apart and bake in the upper third of the oven till golden brown, about 10 minutes. Brush the tops with the melted butter and serve warm.

biscuit bonus

To freeze partially baked biscuits, bake them till just pale, let cool completely, and store in freezer bags up to two weeks. To serve, bake the frozen biscuits in a preheated 425° oven till golden brown, about 15 minutes.

Smoked Salmon and Dill Biscuits with Salmon Caviar

Who says biscuits can't be elegant? Not a certain American chef aboard the *QE2* who once came up with these colorful bite-size canapés for a private cocktail party during a transatlantic voyage. Do look for the freshest smoked salmon, and by no means cheat by using any strong, processed caviar instead of the fresh. Needless to say, this is one biscuit canapé that should be served as soon as it's prepared.

Makes about 1¹/₂ dozen small biscuits

1¹/₂ cups all-purpose flour
2 teaspoons baking powder
¹/₂ teaspoon salt
3 tablespoons chilled butter, cut into bits
2 ounces smoked salmon, minced

2 tablespoons snipped fresh dill
¹/₂ cup heavy cream
Black pepper to taste
Sour cream for topping
Fresh salmon caviar for topping
Fresh dill sprigs for garnish

Basic Scrap Biscuits

I don't really know the reason why, but no matter how carefully and gently you reroll or repat biscuit scraps, the dough never yields the same high, tender biscuits as the mother batch. Usually, I just ignore the frustrating dilemma, aware that the reworking and recutting won't produce perfect results and that most guests couldn't care less. When, on the other hand, I casually make ordinary biscuits for myself and am not forced to meet a quota, what I've learned to do sometimes is simply roll out all the scraps into a thin rectangle, sprinkle finely grated cheese, chopped fresh herbs or olives, minced cooked ham, or crushed nuts over the top, roll it up jelly-roll style, slice it into rounds, and bake them for snacks or to serve when a couple of friends come over for cocktails. Another trick is to blend whatever ingredients you prefer into the scrap dough and form small finger biscuits. To experiment with these biscuits, use the scraps from either Traditional Baking Powder Biscuits (page 10) or Mother's Buttermilk Biscuits (page 12) and bake on an ungreased baking sheet in a preheated 425°F oven till the scraps are golden brown, 10 to 15 minutes, depending on the thickness.

1. Preheat the oven to 425°F.

2. In a large mixing bowl, whisk together the flour, baking powder, and salt. Add the butter and rub it in with your fingertips till the mixture is mealy. Add the smoked salmon, snipped dill, and cream, season with pepper, and stir till the dough is soft.

3. Transfer the dough to a lightly floured work surface and knead about 8 times. Pat out the dough 1/2 inch thick and cut out rounds with a 1¹/₂-inch biscuit cutter. Pat the scraps together and cut out more rounds.

4. Arrange the rounds on a baking sheet about 1/2 inch apart and bake in the center of the oven till golden, about 15 minutes. Let cool completely.

5. Break the biscuits in half, mound a little sour cream onto the soft side of each half, top it with a little caviar, and garnish each with a tiny sprig of dill. Serve immediately.

West Coast Cream Biscuits

Why square cream biscuits seem almost indigenous to the West Coast is baffling, but not only are they the ones James Beard loved to bake in his cooking classes at Seaside, Oregon, but they're the light, creamy biscuits I've noticed most at various parties in Monterey and up in Sonoma Valley. What is different about these biscuits (beside their shape) is the way they're dipped in melted butter before baking. Butter does tend to burn, however, so be extra careful to check the bottoms after about 12 minutes of baking. Served at teas, the biscuits are extraordinary spread lightly with any fruit jam.

Makes at least 1 dozen biscuits

2 cups self-rising flour
1 tablespoon baking powder
1 teaspoon baking soda
$1/2$ teaspoon salt
$1 1/2$ teaspoons sugar
$1 1/4$ cups heavy cream
$1/4$ cup ($1/2$ stick) butter, melted

1. Preheat the oven to 425°F. Grease a baking sheet and set aside.

2. In a large mixing bowl, whisk together the flour, baking powder, baking soda, salt, and sugar. Add the cream and stir constantly till the dough becomes just firm and is no longer sticky.

3. Transfer the dough to a well-floured work surface, knead 4 to 5 times, and pat out into a rectangle about $1/2$ inch thick. Cut out 2-inch squares, then gather up the scraps, pat together, and cut out more squares.

4. Dip both sides of each square into the melted butter, arrange on the prepared baking sheet about 1 inch apart, and bake in the center of the oven till golden, 12 to 14 minutes. Serve warm or at room temperature.

muffins.

2c all purpose flour.
1c sugar.
3 tsp baking powder.
½ tsp salt.
2 eggs.
1 cup milk.
½ veg oil.
1 tsp lemon extract
    (~~the~~ zest on 1 lemon!).
1 cup fresh/frozen
    cranberries, halved.

1. Mix dry.

2. Mix wet.

2. wet → dry. (just
    moistened).

3. fold in cranberries.

    400°, 18·20 min.
    cool 5 min.

Top 5 Burritts

1. Cheddar p37   (not fluffy)
2. Chive   p62 !
3. Sour cream + Dill   p63
4. Parmesean Herb   p 65
5. Rosemary (no garlic) p64.
6. West coast cream   p86
7. Bacon / Onion Scones   p102

Cream Cheese–Jam Biscuits

The inspiration behind these buttery, rich, jam-filled tea biscuits are the "jelly treat" cookies I've been making for decades and serve regularly with ice cream instead of heavy desserts. You can certainly substitute preserves for the jams, so long as the indentations are not cluttered with unsightly chunks or pieces of fruit. While I keep my jelly treats up to 2 or 3 weeks in a tightly closed tin, I don't recommend storing these delicate biscuits more than a few days.

Makes 20 to 24 biscuits

1 1/2 cups all-purpose flour
2 teaspoons baking powder
1/2 teaspoon salt
6 tablespoons (3/4 stick) butter, softened
One 3-ounce package cream cheese, softened
Various fruit jams for fillings

1. Preheat the oven to 425°F. Grease a large baking sheet and set aside.

2. In a large mixing bowl, whisk together the flour, baking powder, and salt till well blended. In a small mixing bowl, combine the butter and cream cheese, stir till well blended, add to the flour, and beat together till you have a smooth well-blended dough.

3. Transfer the dough to a floured work surface and roll into a circle about 1/2 inch thick. Using a floured 1 1/2-inch biscuit cutter, cut out rounds. Roll the scraps together and cut out more rounds. Arrange the rounds on the prepared baking sheet about 1/2 inch apart. Using a floured finger, make a small indentation in the center of each round, spoon a little jam into each indentation (not over-filling it), and bake in the center of the oven till golden, about 12 minutes.

Rolled Cinnamon-Pecan Biscuits

Rolled biscuits seem to have been extremely popular during the early and middle parts of the last century, especially at the quaint ladies' tearooms that flourished in department stores all over the country, as well as at snazzy country clubs. All the old recipes call for the rolled or patted dough to be spread with softened butter or margarine, but some cooks were just as likely to layer the inside with jam, a citrus filling, thinly sliced strawberries, or melted chocolate, as with this traditional spicy nut mixture. One tip: If it's not convenient or appropriate to serve the biscuits warm, store them in a container between sheets of waxed paper till tea time.

Makes about 1 dozen rolled biscuits

^{1}/$_2$ **cup firmly packed light brown sugar**
2 teaspoons ground cinnamon
^{1}/$_2$ **cup finely chopped pecans**
Dough for Mother's Buttermilk Biscuits (page 12)
^{1}/$_4$ **cup (^{1}/$_2$ stick) butter or margarine, softened**

1. Preheat the oven to 425°F. Lightly grease a large baking sheet and set aside.

2. In a small bowl, combine the brown sugar, cinnamon, and pecans, stir till well blended, and set aside.

3. Prepare the biscuit dough and place on a lightly floured work surface. Gently pat the dough out into a rectangle about ^{1}/$_4$ inch thick and spread the softened butter evenly over the top. Sprinkle the sugar mixture evenly over the buttered dough, pressing it in slightly with your fingers. Carefully roll the rectangle up lengthwise into a tight cylinder like a jelly roll, pinch the seam secure, and cut into 1-inch-thick slices with a sharp knife.

4. Arrange the slices on the prepared baking sheet about ^{1}/$_2$ inch apart and bake in the center of the oven till golden brown, about 15 minutes. Serve warm.

Scrap Jelly Biscuits

Since I make dinner and breakfast biscuits regularly, what I might do is collect the scraps from a few batches and store them in a plastic bag in the refrigerator till I have enough dough to make these tasty jelly biscuits that are so perfect for teas. The scraps from any flavored baking powder biscuit dough can be used, and when time comes to make the biscuits, I simply sweeten the dough with a little sugar or honey and grab whatever jars of jelly, jam, marmalade, or fruit preserves might be open. The biscuits are also very good with ice cream.

Scraps of dough from Traditional Baking Powder (page 10), Mother's Buttermilk (page 12), or West Coast Cream Biscuits (page 86)
Jelly, jam, marmalade, or fruit preserves for filling
Egg wash (1 large egg beaten with 1 teaspoon water)

1. Preheat the oven to 425°F. Grease a baking sheet and set aside.

2. Gather up and pat out the scraps of dough about $1/3$ inch thick on a lightly floured work surface and cut out $2^1/2$ x 1-inch rectangles. Make an indentation almost the length of each rectangle and fill each indentation with about $1/2$ teaspoon of jelly. Brush the edges of the rectangles with egg wash.

3. Arrange the rectangles on the prepared baking sheet about $1/2$ inch apart and bake in the upper third of the oven till the biscuits are golden and the jelly bubbling, about 15 minutes. Let the biscuits cool completely, then store in layers separated by waxed paper in an airtight container up to 2 weeks.

The practice of mixing an acid with an alkali to create a leavening agent for biscuits (before the introduction of commercial leavenings) began in the eighteenth century when Colonial cooks probably combined soured milk with sodium bicarbonate (an early form of baking soda) to help breads rise quickly.

Orange Tea Biscuits I

If any recipe demonstrates the fascinating ancestral relationship between the English sweet "biscuit" and its savory American counterpart, this is it. Nothing like these tea biscuits evokes the aura of polite female society as it existed in quaint tea-rooms across America back in the 1920s, '30s, and '40s, and even today in gracious homes of the South and Midwest, such delicate rolled biscuits are almost as popular at afternoon teas as they were in more genteel times. Take care not to saturate this dough with the orange juice and sugar mixture, and spread just enough of the mixture over the tops of the slices to give them a nice glaze.

Makes at least 20 biscuits

2¹/₂ cups all-purpose flour
4 teaspoons baking powder
1 teaspoon salt
¹/₄ cup sugar
¹/₄ cup (¹/₂ stick) chilled butter, cut into bits
1 cup whole milk
2 tablespoons butter, melted
¹/₃ cup orange juice
1 tablespoon grated orange rind

1. Preheat the oven to 450°F. Grease a large baking sheet and set aside.

2. In a large mixing bowl, whisk together the flour, baking powder, salt, and 1 tablespoon of the sugar. Add the chilled butter and rub it in with your fingertips till the mixture is mealy. Add the milk and stir till the dough is soft.

3. Transfer the dough to a lightly floured work surface and knead 3 or 4 times. Pat out the dough into a rectangle ¹/₄ inch thick and brush the melted butter evenly over the top. In a small bowl, combine the remaining 3 tablespoons sugar and the orange juice, stir well, and spread about 2 tablespoons of the mixture evenly over the dough. Sprinkle the orange rind evenly over the top. Roll up the dough lengthwise jelly-roll style, securing the seam, then cut into slices about ¹/₂ inch thick.

4. Arrange the slices cut side down on the prepared baking sheet about 1 inch apart, spread the remaining sugar-and-orange juice mixture over the tops, let stand for 10 minutes, and bake in the center of the oven till golden, 12 to 15 minutes. Let cool and serve at room temperature.

Orange Tea Biscuits II

You don't see sugar cubes very often these days, but forty or fifty years ago it was common practice to dip the cubes in various sweet liquids and use them to glaze the tops of all sorts of delicate baked goods. The cubes certainly do still exist, and while I'm not saying that this technique necessarily produces a better-flavored biscuit than a simple orange syrup brushed on the tops, I can assure you that, for some strange chemical reason, the glaze is one of the prettiest you'll ever see. To make a more tart biscuit, substitute lemon juice and grated lemon peel for the orange.

Makes about 20 biscuits

2 cups all-purpose flour
2 teaspoons baking powder
$1/2$ teaspoon salt
2 tablespoons sugar
$1/4$ cup ($1/2$ stick) chilled butter, cut into bits
1 tablespoon grated orange rind
$2/3$ cup whole milk
10 sugar cubes, cut in half
$1/4$ cup orange juice

1. Preheat the oven to 400°F. Grease a large baking sheet and set aside.

2. In a large mixing bowl, whisk together the flour, baking powder, salt, and sugar. Add the butter and rub it in with your fingertips till the mixture is mealy. Add the orange rind and stir till well blended. Gradually add the milk and stir just till a soft dough forms.

3. Transfer the dough to a lightly floured work surface and knead 3 to 4 times. Roll out the dough $1/2$ inch thick and cut out rounds with a $1^1/2$-inch biscuit cutter. Roll the scraps together and cut out more rounds.

4. Arrange the rounds on the prepared baking sheet. Dip the sugar cube halves briefly into the orange juice, cutting more cubes if necessary. Place a half on top of each round and bake slowly in the center of the oven till the biscuits are nicely glazed, 15 to 20 minutes.

Cinnamon Tea Biscuit Rolls

I consider these elegant little biscuit rolls to be America's updated answer to old-fashioned English tea scones, the creation of a retired countertenor I know in New York who sets one of the most gracious and copious tea tables I've ever witnessed. Of course, the rolls are literally oozing with sweet butter, and you shouldn't hesitate a second to also include a small bowl of fruit preserves to be spread over the tops. Do try to serve these rolls as hot as possible—though they're almost as delicious at room temperature.

Makes about 1 dozen rolls

$1/3$ cup firmly packed light brown sugar

1 teaspoon ground cinnamon

2 cups all-purpose flour

2 teaspoons baking powder

$1/2$ teaspoon salt

$1/2$ cup (1 stick) chilled butter, cut into bits

$2/3$ cup whole milk

Granulated sugar and additional cinnamon and butter for topping

1. Preheat the oven to 425°F. Grease a baking sheet and set aside.

2. On a plate, combine the brown sugar and cinnamon, stir till well blended, and set aside.

3. In a large mixing bowl, whisk together the flour, baking powder, and salt. Add the butter and cut it into the flour with a pastry cutter till the mixture is mealy. Add the milk and stir just till a soft dough forms.

4. Transfer the dough to a lightly floured work surface and knead 3 to 4 times. Roll out the dough about $1/3$ inch thick and cut out 3-inch squares. Fold each square in half, press the top of each half into the prepared sugar-cinnamon mixture, and arrange the halves on the prepared baking sheet about 1 inch apart. Generously sprinkle each half with granulated sugar and additional cinnamon, dot each with additional bits of butter, and bake in the center of the oven till glazed, about 15 minutes. Serve hot or at room temperature.

Scones

There can be no question that the ancestor of the savory American biscuit is the sweet British scone. Exactly when and how the strange transformation of scone to biscuit took place is anybody's guess, but it's for sure that by Colonial times in this country, American cooks had gradually adapted the same technique to make biscuits that the English had used to make scones ever since the early sixteenth century. (And to compound all the confusion, remember that even today in Great Britain the word "biscuit" still refers strictly to either a sweet cookie or an unsweetened cracker.)

Of course, there are a couple of important differences between biscuits and scones besides the sweetness element. First, a scone is almost always thicker than a traditional biscuit and it's certainly not as short in texture or even on top (a true scone, in fact, should look a bit craggy). Less fat (generally butter) is used and rarely chilled, meaning that the consistency of the rubbed flour is more crumbly than mealy, unlike that for biscuits. And the dough is usually stirred till just soft and is not very sticky. Most scones do indeed contain some sugar, but, as a few of the recipes here illustrate, savory scones can be just as delicious as ordinary baking powder biscuits.

Hot from the oven, scones are one of the most distinctive breads ever conceived by man, but be warned that, unlike highly leavened biscuits, most scones tend to be heavy when allowed to cool. To keep them from becoming dry and hard once they're baked, the best idea is to cover them with a clean dish towel till ready to serve.

Plain Scones

I learned to make classic plain scones from none other than Delia Smith, the uncontested queen of modern British cookery, and when I pointed out the uncanny resemblance of her sweet scones to our savory biscuits, even she was surprised. You can stud these scones with everything from dried currants to raisins to chopped nuts, but since they go stale very quickly, they must be served as soon after baking as possible. (If necessary, keep the baked scones warm and soft under a clean dish towel till ready to serve.) Split and spread with fruit preserves or jam, scones are wonderful for both breakfast and teas. They freeze well up to about a month.

Makes about 1 dozen scones

2 cups self-rising flour
1$\frac{1}{2}$ tablespoons superfine sugar
$\frac{1}{2}$ teaspoon salt
2 tablespoons butter, softened
$\frac{3}{4}$ cup whole milk
All-purpose flour for dusting

1. Preheat the oven to 425°F. Lightly grease a large baking sheet and set aside.

2. In a large mixing bowl, whisk together the flour, sugar, and salt, add the butter, and rub very quickly with your fingertips till the mixture is crumbly. Gradually add the milk and stir till a soft dough forms. With floured hands, knead the dough briefly, adding a little more milk if it feels at all dry.

3. Transfer the dough to a lightly floured work surface, roll out not less than $\frac{3}{4}$ inch thick, and cut out rounds with a 2-inch biscuit cutter. Roll the scraps together and cut out more rounds. Arrange the rounds on the prepared baking sheet about $\frac{1}{2}$ inch apart, dust them with a little flour, and bake in the upper third of the oven till golden brown, about 15 minutes.

Orange Cream Scones

The cake flour gives these creamy scones a particularly tender, almost delicate texture, while the orange rind provides just enough tartness to challenge the generous amount of sugar. The wedges are delightful with tea, but I never hesitate to really slather the tops with butter and serve them as warm as possible on a breakfast buffet.

Makes 1 dozen scones

1 1/2 cups all-purpose flour
1 1/2 cups cake flour
1/4 cup sugar
4 teaspoons baking powder
1/2 teaspoon salt
2 large eggs, beaten
1/2 cup heavy cream
2 tablespoons orange juice
2 teaspoons grated orange rind

1. Preheat the oven to 425°F. Grease a baking sheet and set aside.

2. In a large mixing bowl, whisk together both flours, the sugar, baking powder, and salt. Add the eggs, cream, orange juice, and orange rind and stir just till a soft dough forms.

3. Transfer to a lightly floured work surface and knead about 8 times. Divide the dough in half, pat each half into a 6-inch circle, and cut each circle into 6 wedges.

4. Arrange the wedges on the prepared baking sheet about 1/2 inch apart and bake in the center of the oven till golden, about 12 minutes. Butter the tops of the scones lightly and serve warm.

biscuit bonus

For perfect rising and a soft texture, the dough for scones should never be rolled or patted out less than 3/4 inch thick.

Lemon-Date Scones

In many respects, these are the ultimate tea scones, the irony being that, except for the thickness, they're made exactly like many sweetened biscuits. Dates are wonderful in scones, but if you have none on hand, dark or golden raisins work just as well. Do not, on the other hand, substitute milk, half-and half, or even buttermilk for the heavy cream, if you expect a silky soft, rich scone.

Makes about 1 dozen scones

^{1}/$_3$ **cup heavy cream**
2 large eggs
2 tablespoons fresh lemon juice
1 tablespoon grated lemon rind
1^3/$_4$ cups all-purpose flour
2 tablespoons sugar
3 teaspoons baking powder
^{1}/$_2$ **teaspoon salt**
^{1}/$_2$ **cup finely chopped pitted dates**

1. Preheat the oven to 425°F. Grease a baking sheet and set aside.

2. In a small mixing bowl, whisk together the cream and eggs and reserve 1 tablespoon of this mixture. Add the lemon juice and rind to the majority of the mixture and whisk till well blended. In another bowl, whisk together the flour, sugar, baking powder, and salt, add the egg-and-lemon juice mixture and dates, and stir just till a soft dough forms.

3. Transfer to a lightly floured work surface and knead about 8 times. Pat out the dough about ^{3}/$_4$ inch thick and cut out rounds with a 2^1/$_2$-inch biscuit cutter. Pat the scraps together and cut out more rounds. Arrange the rounds on the prepared baking sheet about ^{1}/$_2$ inch apart, brush the tops with the reserved egg mixture, and bake in the center of the oven till golden, about 15 minutes.

Oatmeal-Raisin Scones

Although you want these scones to be slightly crumbly by using minimum liquid in the dough, adding a little cake flour does add a certain delicacy to the texture. The real secret to their mouth-watering flavor is all the butter and, actually, it's not beyond me to gild the lily by cutting a full stick into the dough.

Makes 1 dozen scones

1 cup all-purpose flour
$^1/_2$ cup cake flour
2 teaspoons baking powder
$^1/_2$ teaspoon baking soda
$^1/_2$ teaspoon salt
$^1/_2$ cup firmly packed light brown sugar
6 tablespoons ($^3/_4$ stick) chilled butter, cut into bits
$1^1/_2$ cups old-fashioned oats
$^1/_2$ cup seedless dark raisins
$^1/_2$ cup buttermilk
2 tablespoons butter, melted

1. Preheat the oven to 400°F. Grease a baking sheet and set aside.

2. In a large mixing bowl, whisk together both flours, the baking powder, baking soda, salt, and brown sugar. Add the butter and cut it in with a pastry cutter till the mixture has the texture of oats. Add the oats and raisins and stir till well blended. Add the buttermilk and stir just to moisten the dry ingredients.

3. Transfer the dough to a lightly floured work surface and knead about 8 times. Pat out the dough into a circle about $^3/_4$ inch thick and cut into 12 wedges.

4. Arrange the wedges on the prepared baking sheet about $^1/_2$ inch apart, brush the tops with the melted butter, and bake in the center of the oven till just golden, 12 to 15 minutes.

Spicy Walnut Buttermilk Scones

These rather dense scones are made even more crumbly by the chopped walnuts. I love the texture, but if you prefer something more refined, substitute seedless dark raisins, dried currants, or chopped citrus rind for the nuts. Also feel free to experiment with various spices.

Makes 1 dozen scones

2 cups all-purpose flour
5 tablespoons sugar
3 teaspoons baking powder
$1/2$ teaspoon baking soda
$1/2$ teaspoon salt
$1/2$ cup (1 stick) chilled butter, cut into bits
1 cup buttermilk
$1/2$ cup finely chopped walnuts
1 tablespoon heavy cream
$1/4$ teaspoon ground cinnamon

1. Preheat the oven to 425°F. Grease a baking sheet and set aside.

2. In a large mixing bowl, whisk together the flour, 3 tablespoons of the sugar, the baking powder, baking soda, and salt, add the butter, and work it in quickly with your fingertips till the mixture is crumbly. Add the buttermilk and walnuts and stir just till the dry ingredients are moistened.

3. Transfer the dough to a lightly floured work surface and knead about 8 times. Divide the dough in half, pat each half into a circle about $3/4$ inch thick, and cut each circle into 6 wedges.

4. Arrange the wedges on the prepared baking sheet about $1/2$ inch apart. In a small bowl, combine the cream, cinnamon, and remaining 2 tablespoons sugar, and stir till well blended. Brush the tops of the wedges with the mixture and bake in the center of the oven till golden, 12 to 15 minutes.

Chocolate Chip Scones

Unlike smooth chocolate chip drop cookies, these thick, buttery, hand-formed scones have a fairly rough texture that I find curiously appealing. The dough should be just crumbly and the scones baked a full twenty minutes in a moderate oven. For even richer scones, you can use half-and-half instead of milk, and if you get tired of chocolate chips, substitute dried red currants, chopped candied ginger, or minced crystallized fruits.

biscuit bonus

To make the texture of scones more delicate, add a little cake flour to the all-purpose flour.

Makes 1 dozen scones

2 cups all-purpose flour
2 tablespoons sugar
4 teaspoons baking powder
1 teaspoon salt
1/2 cup (1 stick) chilled butter, cut into pieces
1 cup semisweet chocolate chips
1 cup whole milk

1. Preheat the oven to 350°F. Grease a baking sheet and set aside.

2. In a large mixing bowl, whisk together the flour, sugar, baking powder, and salt. Add the butter and quickly cut it in with a pastry cutter till the mixture is just crumbly. Add the chocolate chips and stir till well blended. Add the milk and stir just till the dry ingredients are moistened.

3. Transfer the dough to a lightly floured work surface and knead 4 to 5 times. With well-floured hands, form the dough into 12 ovals about 1 inch thick. Arrange the ovals on the prepared baking sheet about 1 inch apart and bake in the center of the oven till golden brown, about 20 minutes.

Whole Wheat Fruit Griddle Scones

The British ancestor of these griddle scones is probably the "girdle" scones that housewives used to make on a thick sheet of iron with handles that was placed directly over hot coals. Today, you can certainly use a griddle on top of the stove, but, to tell the truth, my best griddle scones are made in an ordinary black cast-iron skillet that I keep well seasoned. Since you want a tight dough for these scones, very little milk is needed, and no matter what cooking utensil you use, remember that the rounds should be fairly thin so the scones will be crisp on the outside. Margarine is preferable to butter in this recipe, given the tendency of whole wheat to be heavy.

Makes about 2 dozen scones

2 cups whole wheat flour
2 cups all-purpose flour
1 tablespoon baking powder
$1/2$ cup sugar
$1/2$ teaspoon salt
$1/4$ teaspoon ground allspice
$1/4$ teaspoon ground ginger
$1/2$ cup (1 stick) chilled margarine, cut into pieces
$1/2$ cup finely chopped dried fruits
1 large egg, beaten
Milk, if needed
Butter for greasing griddle

1. In a large mixing bowl, whisk together both flours, the baking powder, sugar, salt, and spices. Add the margarine and rub it in quickly with your fingertips till the mixture is crumbly. Add the fruits and stir till well blended. Add the egg and stir till a dough forms, adding a little milk if the dough seems too dry.

2. Transfer the dough to a lightly floured work surface, roll out about $1/4$ inch thick, and cut out rounds with a $2^1/2$-inch biscuit cutter. Roll the scraps together and cut out more rounds.

3. Melt about 1 tablespoon of butter on a heavy griddle or in a medium-size cast-iron skillet over moderate heat and cook about 4 rounds till golden brown and crisp on the outside, about 3 minutes per side. Repeat with more butter and the remaining rounds and serve warm with lots of butter and jam.

Nebraska Cornmeal Scones

Some years ago on a trip to Omaha to research the area's legendary steaks, one night my host brought to the table a basket of what I judged to be big glazed biscuits wrapped in a small towel. "Not biscuits but our cornmeal scones," he corrected, breaking open one to reveal a soft yellowish interior with red specks. I noticed just how short and flaky the bread was, then the subtle richness, and when he began reeling off the ingredients and telling how the scones were made, it dawned on me that basically they were exactly like ordinary savory biscuits I might make with cornmeal. This is still another example of the close relationship between biscuits and scones and, by the way, the buttered scones were sensational with the prime steaks.

Makes about 1 dozen scones

1 cup all-purpose flour
1 cup yellow cornmeal
1 tablespoon baking powder
$^1/_2$ teaspoon baking soda
$^1/_2$ teaspoon salt
3 tablespoons chilled butter, cut into pieces
3 tablespoons chilled lard, cut into pieces
2 tablespoons seeded and minced red bell pepper
2 large eggs
$^3/_4$ cup buttermilk
1 teaspoon water

1. Preheat the oven to 425°F. Grease a baking sheet and set aside.
2. In a large bowl, whisk together the flour, cornmeal, baking powder, baking soda, and salt, add the butter and lard, and rub it in with your fingertips till mealy. Add the bell pepper and stir well.
3. In a small bowl, whisk together one of the eggs and $^1/_2$ cup of the buttermilk, add to the flour mixture, and stir till a soft dough forms.
4. Transfer the dough to a lightly floured work surface and knead about 8 times. Pat out the dough about $^3/_4$ inch thick and cut out rounds with a $2^1/_2$-inch biscuit cutter. Pat the scraps together and cut out more rounds.
5. Arrange the rounds on the prepared baking sheet about $^1/_2$ inch apart. In a small bowl, whisk together the remaining egg and $^1/_4$ cup buttermilk with the water till well blended, brush the tops of the rounds with the mixture, and bake in the center of the oven till golden brown, about 15 minutes.

Yankee Bacon and Onion Scones

Cut into triangles, these savory, lightly glazed scones have been a staple in New England farmhouses and restaurants since Colonial days and are traditionally served with hearty soups, stews, and roasted meats. Bacon and onions always make a wonderful combination, but other possibilities are diced cooked ham and green bell pepper, snipped fresh chives and grated Parmesan, and virtually any chopped nuts and fresh herbs.

Makes about 1 dozen scones

3 strips lean bacon
1 medium-size onion, minced
2 cups all-purpose flour
1 tablespoon baking powder
$1/2$ teaspoon baking soda
$1/2$ teaspoon salt

Black pepper to taste
$1/4$ cup chilled lard, cut into bits
1 cup buttermilk
1 large egg
1 teaspoon water

1. In a skillet, fry the bacon over moderate heat till crisp and drain on paper towels. Add the onion to the skillet, stir till softened, about 2 minutes, and drain on paper towels. Crumble the bacon finely.

2. Preheat the oven to 425°F. Grease a large baking sheet and set aside.

3. In a large mixing bowl, whisk together the flour, baking powder, baking soda, salt, and pepper, add the lard, and work it in with

biscuit bonus

Store opened and even unopened bags of flour and cornmeal in either airtight containers or tightly sealed plastic bags to prevent bug infestation. In addition, it's a good idea to freeze cornmeal since the natural corn oil can become rancid over time.

your fingertips till the mixture is crumbly. Add the crumbled bacon and onion and stir till well blended. Add the buttermilk and stir just till a sticky dough forms.

4. Transfer the dough to a lightly floured work surface, knead 8 to 10 times, and pat into a rectangle ³/₄ inch thick. With a sharp knife, cut the rectangle in half lengthwise, and cut each half crosswise into 6 long narrow triangles.

5. Arrange the triangles on the prepared baking sheet about 1 inch apart. In a small bowl, whisk together the egg and water, brush the tops of the triangles lightly with the mixture, and bake in the center of the oven till just golden, 12 to 15 minutes.

Bisquick was created in the late 1920s by a Pullman dining-car chef who stocked a mixture of flour, leavening, and lard in his icebox so he could make biscuit dough quickly by just adding milk. After a chemist at General Mills solved a few problems about keeping the leavening potent and the shortening fresh over time, the new mix debuted in 1930.

Southern Sweet Potato Drop Scones

Made with mashed baked sweet potatoes, these scones can be traced in Virginia at least back to the early nineteenth century, no doubt a culinary innovation inspired by early English settlers in the region. Since scones, like biscuits, made with sweet potatoes tend to be rather heavy, they should be softened with a little heavy cream and further lightened with an egg. The flavor of these scones is inimitable, and rare is the time I bake sweet potatoes that I don't pop an extra one or two in the oven with the express intention of using the flesh later on to make scones—or biscuits.

Makes about 1 dozen scones

1 1/2 cups all-purpose flour
2 teaspoons baking powder
1/2 teaspoon salt
1/4 cup (1/2 stick) chilled butter, cut into bits
1 cup baked, mashed, and cooled sweet potato
1/4 cup whole milk
2 tablespoons heavy cream
1 large egg, beaten
1/2 cup seedless golden raisins

1. Preheat the oven to 450°F.

2. In a large mixing bowl, whisk together the flour, baking powder, and salt. Add the butter and cut it in with a pastry cutter till crumbly. Add the sweet potato, milk, cream, and egg and stir till a wet dough forms. Add the raisins and stir till well blended.

3. Drop the dough by heaping tablespoons about 1 inch apart on a baking sheet and bake in the center of the oven till golden and slightly crisp, 15 to 18 minutes.

biscuit bonus

For bulkier, softer, moister scones, buttermilk or sour milk is the preferred liquid for making the dough.

Cooking with Biscuits

American cooks have been utilizing biscuit doughs in various dishes ever since the biscuit itself became part of the culinary vernacular. No doubt the original, poorly leavened doughs spread or dropped on leftover stews and savory pies hardly produced the light, flaky crusts that we relish today, but after the introduction of commercial baking soda, baking powder, and yeast in the mid-nineteenth century, it was only a matter of time before biscuit dough was used to create all sorts of amazing dumplings, pie crusts, cobblers, shortcakes, and even exotic breads.

There really is no limit to the ways biscuits and biscuit doughs can be exploited to make or enhance all sorts of sumptuous dishes. While pot pies, cobblers, and shortcakes are, of course, examples of classic biscuit cookery, I've also included here a few other regional concepts that might inspire you to exercise your imagination in the kitchen and come up with both savory and sweet concoctions you never thought possible.

Old-Fashioned Breakfast Biscuits, Sausage, and Gravy

Once was the time when every diner and roadside cafe in America boasted biscuits and sausage with pan gravy for breakfast (or, in the South, biscuits and country ham with redeye gravy). The hearty dish could be wonderful or wretched, depending on the freshness of the biscuits, the quality of the sausage, and the texture and flavor of the gravy—and the same holds true today when, on increasingly rare occasion, you find it on no-nonsense menus. Made properly, there's simply no better breakfast dish— tasty, filling, and soul-warming. Most of the commercial bulk sausage found in supermarkets is a fatty, gristly disgrace (the only national brand I'll touch is Jimmy Dean), so unless you live in the South (where sausage making is still an art and all sorts of respectable products are available), I strongly suggest you grind your own as outlined here. I use only a cast-iron skillet to make this gravy (never a nonstick one) since you want as much sausage debris as possible stuck to the bottom for both flavor and color. Otherwise, you end up with a tasteless, revolting, milky white gravy. I always fry more sausage and make more biscuits than I need since I know guests will gobble them both up (and I love to have extra biscuits to butter and spread with preserves).

Makes 4 to 6 servings, with extra patties and biscuits

Sausage:

3/4 pound boned pork shoulder, chilled

1/4 pound fresh pork fat, chilled

1 teaspoon salt

1/4 teaspoon black pepper

1 teaspoon ground sage

1/2 teaspoon red pepper flakes

1 tablespoon cold water

Biscuits:

1 1/2 cups all-purpose flour

2 teaspoons baking powder

1/2 teaspoon salt

3 tablespoons chilled vegetable shortening

3/4 cup whole milk

Gravy:

1/4 cup (1/2 stick) butter

1/4 cup all-purpose flour

2 1/2 cups milk

Salt and black pepper to taste

1. To make the sausage, cut the pork and pork fat into 2-inch chunks and grind together with the coarse blade, then the fine blade of a meat grinder into a large mixing bowl. Add the remaining ingredients, moisten both hands with the water, and knead the mixture with your hands till well blended and smooth. Form the sausage meat into 8 patties, fry the patties in a large, heavy skillet over moderate heat till nicely browned and cooked through, about 10 minutes. Drain on paper towels, and keep warm on a plate. Set the skillet with the fat aside.

2. Preheat the oven to 425°F.

3. To make the biscuits, whisk together the flour, baking powder, and salt in a large mixing bowl. Add the shortening and cut it in with a pastry cutter or rub with your fingertips till the mixture is mealy. Gradually add the milk and stir just till the dough holds together and is still sticky. Transfer to a lightly floured work surface, knead about 8 times, and form the dough with your hands into 8 smooth rounds about 1 inch thick. Arrange the rounds on a baking sheet about 1 inch apart, bake in the upper third of the oven till golden brown, about 15 minutes, and keep warm.

4. To make the gravy, pour off about half the fat from the skillet, add the butter, and stir over moderate heat till the fats are incorporated, scraping the browned bits off the bottom. Gradually add the flour, stir till it has absorbed the fats, and cook, stirring constantly, till the flour turns golden brown, about 2 minutes. Gradually add the milk, stirring constantly till the gravy is thickened, smooth, and slightly browned. Season with salt and pepper and stir well.

5. To serve, split 4 to 6 of the biscuits in half and place the bottoms on warm serving plates. Top each bottom with a sausage patty, arrange the biscuit tops at an angle, spoon hot gravy over the tops, and serve immediately.

"Biscuits and gravy is a culinary signpost of rural America. Once the city is far behind, this homey dish becomes part of the landscape, served at every roadside café and restaurant, in as many different ways as there are license plates on the cars out front."

—SUSAN HERRMANN LOOMIS, *Farmhouse Cookbook*, 1991

New England Chicken Pot Pie with Biscuit Crust

The best I can determine, all-American chicken pot pie can be traced back to an early New England leftover stew made with a crude biscuit crust in a black iron pot. No doubt my version is much closer to the classic chicken pot pie we know and love today, the one big difference being that the crust is made with a biscuit dough that at least approximates what our ancestors might have had but is delightfully flaky.

Makes 6 servings

Filling:

2 tablespoons butter
2 medium-size onions, diced
1 celery rib, diced
1 large carrot, scraped and diced
3 cups 1-inch cubes cooked chicken
1 1/2 cups fresh or frozen green peas
1 cup diced fresh mushrooms
Salt and black pepper to taste
1/4 cup vegetable shortening
1/4 cup all-purpose flour
1 1/2 cups chicken broth
1 cup half-and-half

Biscuit Crust:

2 cups all-purpose flour
3 teaspoons baking powder
1/2 teaspoon salt
1/4 cup chilled vegetable shortening
1 cup whole milk

1. Grease a 1 1/2-quart flameproof casserole and set aside.

2. To make the filling, melt the butter over moderate heat in a large skillet, add the onions, celery, and carrot, stir till the vegetables soften, about 5 minutes, and scrape into the prepared casserole. Add the chicken, peas, and mushrooms, season with salt and pepper, stir, and set aside.

biscuit bonus

Biscuits tend to have a lighter texture when patted instead of rolled out. Since biscuit dough should be handled as little as possible, folding it over itself and repeatedly patting or rolling out is generally not recommended.

3. In a heavy, medium-size saucepan, melt the shortening over moderate heat, sprinkle the flour over the top, and stir constantly about 3 minutes. Remove from the heat and gradually add the broth and half-and-half, stirring constantly till well blended. Return the mixture to the heat and cook, stirring constantly, till the sauce thickens. Pour over the chicken and vegetables.

4. Preheat the oven to 425°F.

5. To make the biscuit crust, whisk together the flour, baking powder, and salt in a large mixing bowl. Add the shortening and cut it in with a pastry cutter till the mixture is mealy. Add the milk and stir just till the dough forms a ball. Transfer to a lightly floured work surface, knead about 8 times, then pat the dough out about 1/3 inch thick. Cut the dough to fit the top of the casserole, drape it over the filling and secure the edges, and bake till the crust is nicely browned, about 25 minutes.

In the eighteenth century, provisions on a typical New England fishing ship consisted mostly of caught fish, salt pork, molasses, flour, ship's biscuit, water, and rum.

Drop Biscuit–Crusted Chicken and Vegetables

I was first introduced to this simple but utterly delicious casserole by a friend in San Francisco who prided himself on his drop biscuits and used them to enhance all sorts of dishes. Remember that the dough should not cover the top but merely be dropped in little mounds that serve as a crispy counterpoint to the soft chicken and vegetables. The dish is just as good made with leftover turkey and considerably more exotic with roast pheasant or baked rabbit.

Makes 4 to 6 servings

Chicken and Vegetables:

2 tablespoons vegetable shortening

1 medium-size onion, chopped

1 medium-size celery rib, chopped

1 medium-size carrot, scraped and chopped

1 1/2 cups frozen baby lima beans

1/2 cup chicken broth

2 cups milk

1/4 cup all-purpose flour

1 tablespoon finely chopped fresh parsley leaves

Salt and black pepper to taste

2 cups diced cooked chicken

Biscuit Dough:

1 cup all-purpose flour

2 teaspoons baking powder

1 teaspoon dried tarragon, crumbled

1/2 teaspoon salt

2 tablespoons chilled vegetable shortening

1/2 cup whole milk

1. To prepare the chicken and vegetables, melt the shortening over moderate heat in a heavy, flameproof 1 1/2-quart casserole, add the onion, celery, and carrot, and stir till the onion is softened, about 5 minutes. Add the lima beans and broth, bring to a simmer, cover, and cook till the carrot is tender, about 10 minutes. In a bowl, whisk together the milk, flour, and parsley, season with salt

biscuit bonus

When measuring flour in a measuring cup, never pack it down (you'll end up with an ounce too much). Measure flour lightly.

and pepper, add to the vegetables, and stir over moderate heat till the mixture thickens. Add the chicken, stir till well blended, and remove the casserole from the heat.

2. Preheat the oven to 375°F.

3. To make the biscuit dough, whisk together the flour, baking powder, tarragon, and salt in a medium-size mixing bowl. Add the shortening and cut it in with a pastry cutter till the mixture is mealy. Add the milk and stir just till the dough is blended but still very wet. Drop 8 heaping tablespoons of the dough over the top of the casserole and bake till bubbly and the biscuits are browned, about 30 minutes.

"Biscuit for breakfast is a social and economic self-measurement among croppers and hands. Those who always have biscuit for breakfast regard themselves as successful persons of dignity. They pity and look down on the unfortunate who have to go back to corn pone during hard times."

—WILLIAM BRADFORD HUIE, *Mud on the Stars*, 1942

Ham and Mushroom Casserole with Herbed Biscuit Crust

This casserole is delicious just by itself, but top it with a rich biscuit crust and you have something truly sensational to serve on virtually any occasion. What's particularly nice about this recipe is that you can substitute leftover lamb, veal, poultry, and even certain seafoods for the ham with equally satisfying results.

Makes 6 servings

Filling:
1/4 cup (1/2 stick) butter
1 medium-size onion, finely chopped
1 cup diced fresh mushrooms
3 tablespoons all-purpose flour
1/4 teaspoon dry mustard
1 cup milk
1 cup half-and-half
3 cups 1-inch cubes cooked ham
1 cup fresh or frozen green peas
Salt and black pepper to taste

Herbed Biscuit Crust:
2 cups all-purpose flour
1 tablespoon baking powder
1/2 teaspoon salt
1/4 teaspoon ground sage
1/4 teaspoon dried rosemary, crumbled
1/4 cup (1/2 stick) chilled butter
3/4 cup half-and-half

1. Grease a 1 1/2-quart flameproof casserole and set aside.

2. To make the filling, melt the butter over moderate heat in a large, heavy saucepan, add the onion and mushrooms, and stir till the mushrooms begin to yield their liquid, about 5 minutes. Sprinkle the flour and mustard over the vegetables and stir 3 minutes

"As drie as the remainder bisket after a voyage."

—SHAKESPEARE,
As You Like It

longer. Remove the pan from the heat and gradually add the milk and half-and-half, stirring constantly till well blended. Return to the heat and cook, stirring constantly, till the sauce thickens. Add the ham and peas, season with salt and pepper, stir well, transfer the mixture to the prepared casserole, and set aside.

3. Preheat the oven to 425°F.

4. To make the herbed biscuit crust, whisk together the flour, baking powder, salt, sage, and rosemary in a large mixing bowl. Add the butter and cut it in with a pastry cutter till the mixture is mealy. Add the half-and-half and stir just till a ball of dough forms. Transfer to a lightly floured work surface, knead about 8 times, then pat the dough out about 1/3 inch thick. Cut the dough to fit the top of the casserole, drape it over the filling and secure the edges, and bake till the crust is browned, about 25 minutes.

Country ham biscuits are still a cocktail staple of the South. As Betty Fussell writes so aptly in *I Hear America Cooking* (1986), "the biscuits are short, small as a quarter, thin as a dime, split in two, buttered, layered with a thin slice of country ham, put back together, and eaten by the bushel and the peck.

Biscuit Dumplings

In the South, chicken and dumplings are also called chicken and pastry, and in North Carolina, the dish is often referred to as "chicken slick." Whatever the term, biscuit dumplings are dropped into not only numerous braised chicken preparations but also virtually any stew or thick soup that contains sufficient liquid for poaching the nuggets of dough. Sometimes the dumplings are very peppery, sometimes slightly herby, but rarely are they not sweetened a bit to create an interesting contrast with the savory broth in which they're cooked.

Makes about 20 biscuit dumplings

1¹/2 cups all-purpose flour
1 tablespoon baking powder
1 teaspoon sugar
1 teaspoon salt
¹/2 teaspoon black pepper

2 tablespoons chilled lard, cut into
    small pieces
1 cup whole milk
1 large egg, beaten

1. In a large mixing bowl, whisk together the flour, baking powder, sugar, and salt and pepper. Add the lard and rub it in with your fingertips till the mixture is mealy. Add the milk and egg and stir till the dough is soft but still almost wet.

2. Drop the dough by heaping tablespoons into boiling soup or stew liquid, reduce the heat to moderate, cover, and simmer till the dumplings are tender, about 15 minutes.

Today's oyster crackers dropped or crumbled into Yankee chowders most probably evolved from the eighteenth- and nineteenth-century "ship's biscuit," which was used to thicken chowders before cubed potatoes became a main ingredient.

Oyster Pie with Biscuit Crust

Cotuits from Nantucket Sound, Wellfleets from Cape Cod, Chincoteagues from Virginia, Bluepoints from Long Island, Olympias from Washington State—the varieties and wide availability of coastal oysters in the U. S. over the past two centuries have been the inspiration behind some of our most renowned dishes, not the least of which are the different styles of oyster pie found throughout the country. Most today are made with a pretty bland, ordinary pie dough, but in the South and throughout much of New England, cooks still produce a crisp, buttery crust by dropping biscuit dough all over the top just as their ancestors did. This, in my opinion, is oyster pie in all its true glory.

Makes 4 to 6 servings

Oyster Filling:

1/4 cup (1/2 stick) butter

2 tablespoons minced onion

3 tablespoons all-purpose flour

1 cup half-and-half

1 pint fresh shucked oysters, 1/4 cup of their liquor reserved

1 teaspoon fresh lemon juice

Salt and black pepper to taste

Tabasco sauce to taste

Biscuit Crust:

1 1/4 cups all-purpose flour

2 teaspoons baking powder

1/2 teaspoon salt

3 tablespoons chilled butter, cut into bits

1/2 cup whole milk

1. Preheat the oven to 400°F.

2. To make the pie, melt the butter in a medium-size saucepan over moderate heat, add the onion, and stir till softened, about 1 minute. Add the flour and stir for 1 minute. Gradually add the half-and-half and stir till the mixture thickens. Add the reserved oyster liquor and lemon juice, season with salt, pepper, and Tabasco, reduce the heat to low, and stir for 1 minute. Add the oysters and stir till their edges begin to curl, about 4 minutes. Scrape into a 9-inch pie plate and set aside.

3. To make the biscuit crust, whisk together the flour, baking powder, and salt in a medium-size mixing bowl. Add the butter and cut it in with a pastry cutter till the mixture is mealy. Add the milk and stir just till the dough holds together but is still slightly wet. Drop the biscuit dough by tablespoons over the entire surface of the pie and bake in the center of the oven till the crust is golden brown, about 30 minutes.

Texas Chili on Jalapeño Buttermilk Biscuits

I was first exposed to the idea of chili con carne spooned over spicy buttermilk biscuits at a real Tex-Mex dive in San Antonio, and to this day I still think this is the greatest way on earth to eat chili. While you should by all means feel free to use your own chili recipe, I do strongly advise that you not tamper too much with the biscuit recipe if you want what I consider to be the perfect biscuit texture for this dish; it's essential, for example, that you not substitute another fat for the lard.

Makes 6 servings

Chili:
$^1/_4$ cup vegetable oil
2 large onions, chopped
1 large green bell pepper, seeded and chopped
2 garlic cloves, minced
3 pounds ground beef chuck
$^1/_4$ cup chili powder
1 tablespoon ground cumin
1 tablespoon dried oregano, crumbled
1 tablespoon red pepper flakes
One 18-ounce can tomato sauce
1 cup water
One 15.5-ounce can pinto beans, drained
Salt and black pepper to taste

Jalapeño Buttermilk Biscuits:
2 cups all-purpose flour
1 tablespoon baking powder
$^1/_2$ teaspoon baking soda
1 teaspoon salt
$^1/_4$ cup chilled lard, cut into pieces
2 small jalapeño chiles, seeded and minced
1 cup buttermilk

1. Preheat the oven to 425°F.

2. To make the chili, heat the oil over moderate heat in a large, heavy pot or skillet, add the onions, bell pepper, and garlic, and stir till the vegetables are softened, about 3 minutes. Add the beef and cook, stirring and breaking up any lumps, till it is no longer pink,

about 10 minutes. Add the chili powder, cumin, oregano, and pepper flakes and stir for 1 minute. Add the tomato sauce, water, and beans, season with salt and pepper, bring to a boil, reduce the heat to low, cover, and simmer for 1 hour, stirring from time to time.

3. To make the biscuits, whisk together the flour, baking powder, baking soda, and salt in a large mixing bowl. Add the lard and rub it in with your fingertips till the mixture is mealy. Add the jalapeños and buttermilk and stir till just blended but still sticky. Transfer the dough to a lightly floured work surface and knead about 8 times. Pat out the dough 1/2 inch thick and cut out rounds with a 3-inch biscuit cutter. Pat the scraps together and cut out more rounds. Arrange them on a large baking sheet about 1 inch apart and bake in the center of the oven till golden, about 15 minutes.

4. To serve, split the biscuits in half, arrange two halves on each plate, and spoon the chili over the tops.

"Let one spend the night at some gentleman-farmer's home and the first sound heard in the morning, after the crowing of the cock, was the heavy, regular fall of the cook's axe, as she beat and beat her biscuit dough."

—MARY STUART SMITH, *Virginia Cookery-Book*, 1885

Saddleback Liver and Onions

New Jersey still has some of the best old-fashioned diners in the nation, and when two friends and I stopped at one for lunch on our way down to Princeton from New York and I noticed liver and onions on the laminated menu, I asked the waitress exactly how they were served. "We just call it 'saddle-back,'" she sort of mumbled, "spooned over our butter biscuits. It's good. You'll like it." And, indeed, I did—very much. This is my version, and I like to serve the dish at very casual dinners with no more than a big tossed salad and either red wine or beer. You don't want the liver and onions to be too soupy, so start with only about 1½ cups of broth and add more as needed to produce a very moist but firm texture. Be sure not to overcook the liver and toughen it.

Makes 4 servings

Biscuits:

2 cups all-purpose flour
1 tablespoon baking powder
1 teaspoon salt
¼ cup (½ stick) chilled butter, cut into bits
1 cup whole milk

Liver and Onions:

1½ pounds thin calf's liver, trimmed of membranes and cut into ¼-inch strips
¼ cup all-purpose flour
Salt and black pepper to taste
¼ cup vegetable oil
3 medium-size onions, thinly sliced
2 cups beef broth
1 tablespoon bacon grease

1. Preheat the oven to 425°F.

2. To make the biscuits, whisk together the flour, baking powder, and salt in a large mixing bowl. Add the butter and rub it in with your fingertips till the mixture is mealy. Add the milk and stir till just blended. Transfer the dough to a lightly floured work surface and

biscuit bonus

For soft, fluffy biscuits, place them close together on the baking sheet. For crusty ones, place about one inch apart.

knead about 8 times. Pat out the dough $1/4$ inch thick, cut into 8
rounds with a 3-inch biscuit cutter, arrange them on a large baking
sheet about $1/2$ inch apart, and bake in the center of the oven till
golden, 12 to 15 minutes.

3. Meanwhile, combine the liver strips, flour and salt and pepper in
   a large mixing bowl and toss to coat the liver. In a large, heavy
   skillet, heat 2 tablespoons of the oil over moderately high heat,
   add the liver, brown on all sides, and transfer to another bowl.
   Add the remaining 2 tablespoons oil to the skillet, reduce the heat
   to moderate, add the onions, and stir till golden, 8 to 10 minutes.
   Add the broth, bacon grease, and liver and simmer till the liver is
   cooked through, about 10 minutes.

4. To serve, split the biscuits in half and spoon the liver and onions
   over the tops. Serve immediately.

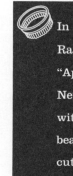 In *The Virginia Housewife* of 1836, Mary
Randolph writes of a beaten biscuit called
"Apoquiniminc cake," named after a town in
New Castle County, Delaware. The biscuit is made
with flour, butter, egg, and milk, and the dough is
beaten with a pestle for 30 minutes before being
cut into rounds and baked on a gridiron.

Leek, Tomato, and Mushroom Biscuit Pizzas

One advantage to making pizzas with unorthodox biscuit dough is that no yeast is involved as with traditional pizza dough, meaning you don't have to wait around for the dough to rise. Of course, the baking powder does leaven the dough nicely, and adding the olive oil to the dough produces a mellow crust that is crisp but firm enough to accommodate the liquidy topping. The pizzas can also be cut into wedges for appetizers.

Makes two 8-inch pizzas; 2 main-course servings or 4 to 6 appetizer servings

Topping:

2 tablespoons olive oil

1 large leek (white part and some of the green included), washed well, thinly sliced crosswise, and patted dry

1 large ripe tomato, peeled, seeded, and chopped

$1/4$ pound fresh mushrooms, thinly sliced

$1/2$ teaspoon dried oregano, crumbled

$1/2$ teaspoon red pepper flakes

$1/2$ teaspoon salt, or to taste

Black pepper to taste

Biscuit Crust:

2 tablespoons olive oil

$1/4$ cup whole milk

1 cup all-purpose flour

1 teaspoon baking powder

$1/4$ cup ($1/2$ stick) chilled butter, cut into bits

6 ounces mozzarella cheese, shredded

1. To make the topping, in a medium-size, heavy skillet, heat the olive oil over moderate heat, add the leek, tomato, and mushrooms, and stir for about 5 minutes. Add the oregano and red pepper flakes, season with salt and black pepper, stir till the vegetables are very soft, about 5 minutes longer, and remove from the heat.

biscuit bonus

Baking powder might make biscuits rise to impressive heights, but too much can impart a chemical taste and make the biscuits dry.

2. Preheat the oven to 450°F.

3. To make the biscuit crust, in a small bowl, whisk together the olive oil and milk till well blended. In a medium-size mixing bowl, whisk together the flour, baking powder, and salt. Add the butter and rub it in with your fingertips till the mixture is mealy. Add the oil-and-milk mixture and stir just till a soft dough forms. Transfer to a lightly floured work surface, knead about 8 times, cut the dough in half, and roll each half into an 8-inch round. Arrange the two rounds on a large baking sheet and form a $1/4$-inch rim around the edges.

4. Spoon equal amounts of the vegetable mixture over the rounds, sprinkle equal amounts of cheese over the tops, and bake the pizzas till the crusts are golden and crisp, about 15 minutes.

"Although she [Alice B. Toklas] remains staunchly American in spite of fifty years in France, you have the feeling that she has forgotten some of our more colloquial eating habits. The hot baking-powder-biscuit mix did not intrigue her. She referred to it in her letter as the 'yeast' biscuits, and said, 'They can't save more than ten minutes. Is it that worth while?'"

—POPPY CANNON, Introduction to *Arrows and Flavors* (1958) by Alice B. Toklas

Old-Fashioned Strawberry Shortcake

Authentic American strawberry shortcake is not, repeat *not*, made with those small, overly sweet, commercial sponge cakes, but rather with rich, warm, split biscuits that have been either buttered or lightly glazed with cream before being adorned with the ripest of fresh strawberries and cold vanilla-flavored, real whipped cream—none of that Cool Whip nonsense, mind you. Great strawberry shortcake like our ancestors made is quick and easy to prepare, so there's absolutely no excuse in settling for anything less. The contrast between the warm, crusty biscuits, softly juicy berries, and cold whipped cream is literally indescribable. If, when you split the biscuits open, you feel like slathering butter over the halves, go right ahead.

Makes 6 to 8 shortcakes

Shortcake:

2 cups self-rising flour

$1/4$ cup sugar

$1/2$ cup (1 stick) chilled butter, cut into bits

$1/3$ cup half-and-half, plus more for brushing

1 large egg, beaten

Topping:

3 cups hulled and sliced ripe strawberries

$1/4$ cup sugar

1 cup heavy cream

$1/4$ teaspoon pure vanilla extract

1. Preheat the oven to 425°F. Grease a large baking sheet and set aside.

2. To make the shortcake, mix together the flour and sugar in a large mixing bowl. Add the butter and cut it in with a pastry cutter till the mixture is crumbly. Add the half-and-half and egg and stir just till the dry ingredients are moistened. Transfer the dough to a lightly floured work surface and knead 3 to 4 times. Roll out the dough $1/2$ inch thick, cut out rounds with a $2 1/2$-inch biscuit cutter,

and arrange on the prepared baking sheet. Roll the scraps together and cut out more rounds. Brush the tops lightly with half-and-half and bake in the upper third of the oven till golden brown, 12 to 15 minutes.

3. Meanwhile, make the topping by tossing the strawberries and sugar together in a medium-size mixing bowl. In another medium-size mixing bowl, beat together the cream and vanilla with an electric mixer till thick but still soft and refrigerate till ready to use.

4. Split the hot biscuits in half, spoon equal amounts of strawberries over the bottom halves, spoon the flavored whipped cream over the strawberries, and cover with the biscuit tops at an angle. Serve immediately.

In Mary Lincoln's *Boston Cook Book* of 1883, the ingredients for a griddle shortcake (i.e., strawberry shortcake) included flour, baking soda, cream of tartar, salt, sweet butter, and soured milk, along with bowls of sweetened sliced fresh strawberries and cream. The biscuits were to be browned slowly in butter on a grill, split open, and lavished with strawberries, strawberry juice, and plenty of cream.

Spiced Peach Shortcake

I must say I love this spicy summer shortcake as much as one made with strawberries, serving it regularly when the first luscious freestone Southern peaches come on the market in late June or early July. Just be extremely careful not to overcook the peaches; they should be perfectly softened and never mushy. Likewise, the biscuits should be soft inside and just crusty enough to provide a textural contrast to the soft peaches and whipped cream.

Makes 6 shortcakes

Topping:

5 medium-size ripe but firm peaches, peeled, pitted, and cut into $1/2$-inch pieces

$1/2$ cup firmly packed light brown sugar

$1/4$ teaspoon ground cinnamon

$1/8$ teaspoon ground nutmeg

$1/8$ teaspoon pure almond or vanilla extract

2 teaspoons fresh lemon juice

Shortcake:

2 cups all-purpose flour

1 tablespoon baking powder

2 tablespoons granulated sugar

$1/2$ teaspoon salt

$11/4$ cups heavy cream

Milk for brushing

Whipped cream for topping

1. To make the topping, in a large, heavy saucepan combine the peaches, brown sugar, cinnamon, nutmeg, almond extract, and lemon juice and stir till well blended. Bring the mixture to a simmer, cover, and cook over medium-low heat till the peaches are just soft, about 10 minutes. Remove from the heat and let cool.

2. Meanwhile, preheat the oven to 425°F.

3. To make the shortcake, in a large mixing bowl, whisk together the flour, baking powder, granulated sugar, and salt, add the cream, and stir just till a soft dough forms. Transfer the dough to a lightly floured work surface and knead about 8 times. Pat out the dough $1/2$ inch thick and cut out rounds with a 3-inch biscuit cutter. Pat the scraps together and cut out more rounds till there are 6 in all. Arrange the rounds on a large baking sheet about 1 inch apart, brush the tops with milk, and bake in the center of the oven till golden, about 15 minutes. Let the biscuits cool.

4. Split the biscuits in half, arrange the bottom halves split side up on 6 dessert plates, and mound equal amounts of the peaches on top of each. Top each mound with the other biscuit half and a generous dollop of whipped cream. Serve immediately.

"A bite of real strawberry shortcake . . . is a mouthful of contrasts. The rich, sweet cream, the tart juicy berries, and the sour, crumbly texture of hot biscuits all refuse to amalgam into a single flavor tone, but produce mouth-stimulating contrasts of flavor—hot and cold, soft and hard, sweet and tart, smooth and crumbly."

—JOHN THORNE, *Simple Cooking*, 1987

All-Purpose Biscuit Dough for Fruit Cobblers

Use this dough for any fruit cobbler that calls for a buttery top crust. For a less rich but fluffier crust, substitute vegetable shortening for the butter, and for the most tender and flakiest topping, use lard. The dough can be dropped over the fruit as directed here, or it can be stirred more till slightly firmer and spread evenly over the top.

Makes enough dough to top a 12 x 9-inch cobbler

1$\frac{1}{2}$ cups all-purpose flour
2 teaspoons baking powder
$\frac{1}{2}$ teaspoon salt
$\frac{1}{4}$ teaspoon baking soda
$\frac{1}{2}$ cup sugar
$\frac{1}{4}$ cup ($\frac{1}{2}$ stick) chilled butter, cut into small pieces
1 cup buttermilk or plain yogurt (don't use lowfat or nonfat)

1. In a mixing bowl, whisk together the flour, baking powder, salt, baking soda, and sugar. Add the butter and rub it in with your fingertips till the mixture is mealy. Add the buttermilk and stir just till the dough is wet.

2. Drop the dough by tablespoons over the fruit just before baking.

Coffee Cake Biscuits

When you make the dough for these clever biscuits, which are so unusual on a breakfast or brunch buffet, be sure to cut out the rounds about ³/₄ inch thick so they'll resemble plump little coffee cakes. The hostess on Long Island who introduced me to them served two different jams to be spread over the tops, but, frankly, I think the biscuits stand very well on their own. Sometimes I do like to use half granulated sugar and half light brown in the nut mixture for added flavor. Serve these biscuits as hot as possible direct from the baking dish.

Makes 1 dozen coffee cake biscuits

¹/₂ **cup finely chopped walnuts**
¹/₂ **cup sugar**
1¹/₂ **teaspoons ground cinnamon**
12 **unbaked Sour Milk Biscuit (page 19), Clabber Biscuit (page 21) or Butter-Yogurt Biscuit (page 24) rounds**

1. Preheat the oven to 425°F. Butter a large, shallow baking dish and set aside.

2. On a plate, combine the walnuts, sugar, and cinnamon and stir till very well blended. Carefully dip both sides of the biscuit rounds into the melted butter, then the pecan mixture, and arrange them in the prepared baking dish about ¹/₂ inch apart. Bake in the center of the oven till golden brown, 12 to 15 minutes. Serve hot.

James Beard's Blueberry Grunt

James Beard had a way with fruit cobblers, crisps, grunts, and crumbles like nobody I ever knew, and I'll never forget this particular spicy grunt made with molasses and dropped biscuit dough he once made for lunch in the outdoor garden of his town house in New York. Jim said the recipe was his mother's and, for both ultimate flavor and texture, he insisted on using both butter and shortening in his biscuit dough. He liked the grunt so hot that vanilla ice cream began to melt the second it was dolloped on top of each portion. The dessert is just as memorable made with fresh blackberries.

Makes 4 to 6 servings

Filling:

3 cups fresh blueberries, picked over
   for stems and rinsed
$1/3$ cup sugar
$1/4$ teaspoon ground cinnamon
$1/4$ teaspoon ground nutmeg
$1/4$ teaspoon ground cloves
$1/4$ cup unsulfured molasses
2 tablespoons fresh lemon juice

Biscuit Crust:

1 cup all-purpose flour
$1^{1}/2$ teaspoons baking powder
$1/4$ teaspoon salt
3 tablespoons chilled butter
1 tablespoon chilled vegetable
   shortening
1 large egg, beaten
$1/3$ cup whole milk

1. Preheat the oven to 375°F.

2. To make the filling, butter a deep 9-inch pie plate and spread the berries evenly over the bottom. Sift the sugar and spices together over the berries, dribble the molasses evenly over the top, and sprinkle with the lemon juice. Bake till the berries begin to render their juice, about 5 minutes, remove the plate from the oven, and increase the oven temperature to 425°F.

3. To make the biscuit crust, whisk together the flour, baking powder, and salt in a medium-size mixing bowl. Add the butter and shortening and cut them in with a pastry cutter till the mixture is mealy. Add the egg and milk and stir just till a very soft dough forms, adding a little more milk if necessary. Drop the dough by tablespoons over the berries, spread it evenly to cover them, and bake till the crust is nicely browned, about 20 minutes. Serve the grunt topped with vanilla ice cream or heavy cream.

Onion Biscuit Bread

Simply put, this is an amazing biscuit bread that I love to serve with chopped pork barbecue, Brunswick stew, and grilled meats when I'm too lazy to make hush puppies. Test the bread carefully with a toothpick to make sure it is fully firm, which might require a few more minutes of baking. The bread freezes beautifully, either before or after baking, so you might think about making two loaves.

Makes 1 loaf

2 cups self-rising flour

$^1/_2$ teaspoon black pepper

$^1/_4$ cup chilled vegetable shortening

$1^1/_2$ cups whole milk

2 tablespoons butter or margarine

3 medium-size onions, finely chopped

1 large egg

1 tablespoon cornstarch

1. Preheat the oven to 450°F. Grease a 16 x 9-inch baking pan and set aside.

2. In a large mixing bowl, combine the flour and pepper. Add the shortening and cut it in with a pastry cutter till the bits are the size of small peas. Add 1 cup of the milk, stir just till blended, and set aside.

3. In a large, heavy skillet, melt the butter over moderate heat, add the onions, and stir till golden, about 10 minutes. Add the onions to the flour mixture.

4. In a small mixing bowl, whisk together the remaining $^1/_2$ cup milk, the egg, and cornstarch, add to the flour-onion mixture, and stir till well blended and still moist. Scrape the dough into the prepared baking pan, smooth the top with a rubber spatula, and bake till a toothpick inserted in the center comes out clean, 20 to 25 minutes. Cut the loaf into squares and serve warm.

Jean's Sticky Biscuits

My long-time friend, colleague, and fellow Southerner, Jean Anderson, relates in her wonderful *American Century Cookbook* how her mother came up with this delightful variation on old-fashioned sticky buns as a way to avoid having to fool with yeast dough. Contrary to what the long list of ingredients might imply, the biscuits are quick and easy and perfect for a stylish brunch.

Makes 9 biscuits

Glaze:
$1/4$ cup ($1/2$ stick) butter
$1/2$ cup orange juice
$1/2$ cup firmly packed light brown sugar
1 tablespoon finely grated orange rind

Biscuits:
2 cups all-purpose flour
1 tablespoon baking powder
$1/2$ teaspoon salt
$1/4$ cup vegetable oil
$3/4$ cup whole milk

Filling:
$1/4$ cup firmly packed light brown sugar
$1/2$ teaspoon ground cinnamon
$1/4$ teaspoon ground allspice

1. Grease an 8-inch square baking pan. In a small, heavy saucepan, bring the glaze ingredients to a boil, spoon the mixture into the prepared pan so it completely covers the bottom, and set aside.

2. Preheat the oven to 450°F.

3. To make the biscuits, whisk together the flour, baking powder,
and salt in a large mixing bowl and make a well in the center.
In a small mixing bowl, whisk together the oil and milk till well
blended, pour into the well, and stir just till a soft dough forms.
Transfer the dough to a lightly floured work surface and roll into
an 18 x 10-inch rectangle.

4. In a small mixing bowl, mix together the filling ingredients, then
sprinkle evenly over the rectangle. Starting from the short side, roll
up the rectangle jelly-roll style into an 18-inch-long log, slice into 9
biscuits 2 inches thick, arrange the biscuits cut side down in 3 rows
in the glazed pan, and bake till puffed and golden brown, about 20
minutes.

5. Invert the pan immediately onto a large platter so the glaze runs
down over the biscuits and serve hot.

 Canned biscuits were perfected in the 1930s
by a Louisville baker, who sold the idea to
Ballard Flour Company. After Pillsbury
eventually took over Ballard, refrigerated
"popping" dough was introduced to the
nation in 1953. Today, Pillsbury sells no less
than 276 million cans of biscuits per year—
that's 2.5 billion biscuits!

Mail-Order Sources for Soft-Wheat Flour

King Arthur Flour Company Baker's Catalogue
P.O. Box 876
Norwich, VT 05055
(800) 827-6836
www.kingarthurflour.com
Order the soft-wheat pastry flour for biscuit making.

Martha White Foods
200 Butler Drive
Murfreesboro, TN 37133
(800) 663-6317
www.marthawhite.com

White Lily Foods
P.O. Box 871
Knoxville, TN 37901
(800) 264-5459
www.whitelily.com

Index